Media Law in Montenegro

Media Law in Montenegro

Aneta Spaić

This book was originally published as a monograph in the International Encyclopaedia of Laws/Media Law.

Founding Editor: Roger Blanpain
General Editor: Frank Hendrickx
Volume Editors: Peggy Valcke & Eva Lievens

Wolters Kluwer

Published by:
Kluwer Law International B.V.
PO Box 316
2400 AH Alphen aan den Rijn
The Netherlands
Website: www.wolterskluwerlr.com

Sold and distributed in North, Central and South America by:
Wolters Kluwer Legal & Regulatory U.S.
7201 McKinney Circle
Frederick, MD 21704
United States of America
Email: customer.service@wolterskluwer.com

Sold and distributed in all other countries by:
Quadrant
Rockwood House
Haywards Heath
West Sussex
RH16 3DH
United Kingdom
Email: international-customerservice@wolterskluwer.com

Printed on acid-free paper

ISBN 978-90-411-8912-7

e-Book: ISBN 978-90-411-8941-7
web-PDF: ISBN 978-90-411-8982-0

This title is available on www.kluwerlawonline.com

Printed and Bound by CPI Group (UK) Ltd, Croydon, CR0 4YY.

The Author

Aneta Spaić was born on September 27, 1981 in Nikšić. She holds a Diploma of International Baccalaureate from the United World College in Trieste, Italy. In 2004, she graduated from the Law Faculty in Podgorica, graduating with top honors (having an average grade of ten). While studying, she was awarded by the city of Podgorica, School of Law and University, several awards and the Charter of the University of Montenegro as best student of the University and Law School. After her Bachelor's in Law, she pursued her Master's in Law at Kyushu University (Fukuoka, Japan) as a scholar of the Japanese Government. In 2004, she was elected for a teaching assistant job and worked as the administrative assistant at the Centre for Human Rights. About the same time, she became a laureate of the Montenegrin Academy of Science and Art. In 2009, she obtained her PhD from the Law Faculty of University of Montenegro in Podgorica. In December of the same year, she was elected for arbitrator of the International Arbitration Court attached to Chamber of Commerce, and she was conferred the academic title of assistant professor at the University of Montenegro. In 2010, she was appointed as the national correspondent by the Government of Montenegro in UNCITRAL. In 2011, she became a member of Centre for Young Scientists of Montenegrin Academy of Science and Art, and in 2014, a member of Global Young Academy. In May 2015, she was conferred the rank of associate professor at University of Montenegro. She gave lectures/speeches on various business legal issues ranging from arbitration, privacy rights, and business financial reform from 2000 to 2014 in a variety of forums from Washington DC to Dallas, Texas to New York, and countries such as Austria, Belgrade, Croatia, Germany, Montenegro, Netherlands, and Spain. In addition, she has the experience of teaching Law in law schools and undergraduate forums, having taught International Business Law at Washington and Lee Law School, Lexington, VA. She is the (co)author of monographs entitled *Commercial and Economic Law in Montenegro* published by Kluwer International, *New Lex Mercatoria and Termination of Sale Contract*, *Mediation in Commercial Disputes*, *Legal Aspects of Mitigating Risks in Project Finance* and writer of significant

The Author

number of articles in both international and national scientific, professional journals. Her areas of interest are: Media Law, EU Law, International Business Law, International Contract Law, and International Commercial Arbitration.

Table of Contents

Table of Contents

Table of Contents

List of Abbreviations

Legislation

BL	Broadcasting Law (OG of MNE, Nos. 51/02, 62/02, 46/04, 56/04)
CC	Criminal Code (OG of MNE, Nos. 70/03, 13/04, 47/06, 40/08, 25/10, 32/11, 64/11, 40/13, 56/13, 14/15)
CM	Constitution of Montenegro (OG of MNE, Nos. 01/07, 38/13)
DBL	Digital Broadcasting Law (OG of MNE, Nos. 34/11, 31/12)
DEMIP	Decision on the List of Events of Major Importance for the Public in Montenegro (OG of MNE, No. 11/12)
DLEMI	Decision on the List of Events of Major Importance for the Public in Montenegro (OG of MNE, No. 11/12)
ECTT	Law on Ratification of the European Convention on Transfrontier Television (OG of MNE, No. 01/08)
EL	Electoral Law (OG of MNE, No. 4/98)
FL	Foreigners Law (OG of MNE, Nos. 82/2008 and 72/09)
LAA	Law on Accounting and Auditing (OG of MNE, Nos. 69/05, 80/08 and 32/11)
LAD	Law on Administrative Disputes (OG of MNE, No. 60/03)
LAEL	Law on Amendments of Electoral Law (Law on Election of Councillors and Members) (OG of MNE, Nos. 04/98, 05/98, 17/98, 14/00, 18/00, 09/01, 41/02, 46/02, 45/04, 48/06, 56/06, 46/11, 14/14, 47/14)
LB	Law on Banks (OG of MNE, Nos. 17/08, 44/10, and 40/11)
LBLIC	Law on Bankruptcy and Liquidation of Insurance Companies (OG of MNE, No. 11/07)
LBO	Law on Business Organizations (OG of MNE, Nos. 06/02, 17/07, 80/08, 40/10, and 40/11)
LBP	Law on Bankruptcy Proceedings (OG of MNE, No. 11/0)
LC	Law on Courts (OG of MNE, No. 11/15)
LCB	Law on Central Bank (OG of MNE, Nos. 40/10, 46/10, and 6/13)
LCivP	Law on Civil Procedure (OG of MNE, No. 22/04)
LCP	Law on Criminal Procedure (OG of MNE, No. 79/09)

LCRR	Law on Copyright and Related Rights (OG of MNE, No. 37/11)
LCT	Law on Contract and Torts (OG of MNE, No. 47/08)
LDoGID	Law on Designations of Origin, Geographical Indications and Designations of Guaranteed Traditional Specialty Agricultural Products and Foodstuffs (OG of MNE, No. 18/11)
LEC	Law on Electronic Communications (OG of MNE, No. 40/13)
LEG	Law on Enforcement and Guarantee (OG of MNE, No. 36/11)
LEM	Law on Electronic Media (OG of MNE, Nos. 46/10, 40/11, 53/11, 055/16)
LEPM	Law on the Election of the President of Montenegro (OG of MNE, Nos. 17/07, 08/09)
LEWF	Law on Employment and Work of Foreigners (OG of MNE, Nos. 22/08 and 32/11)
LFAI	Law on Free Access to Information (OG of MNE, No. 44/12)
LFIL	Law on Foreign Investment Law (OG of MNE, Nos. 82/08, 72/09, 32/11)
LFL	Law on Financial Leasing (OG of MNE, No. 81/05)
LFP	Law on Financing of Political Parties (OF of MNE, Nos. 42/11, 60/11, 1/12)
LFP	Law on Financing Political Parties (OG of MNE, No. 49/08)
LFPSEC	Law on Financing Political Subjects and Electoral Campaigning (OG of MNE, No. 52/14)
LGAP	Law on General Administrative Procedure (OG of MNE, No. 60/03)
LGC	Law on Games of Chance (OG of MNE, Nos. 52/04, 13/07)
LGI	Law on Geographical Indications (OG of MNE, No. 48/08)
LL	Labour Law (OG of MNE, Nos. 49/08, 26/09, 59/11 and 66/12)
LLLE	Law On Liability Of Legal Entities For Criminal Offenses (OG of MNE, No. 70/03, 13/04)
LLPID	Law on Legal Protection of Industrial Designs (OG of MNE, No. 27/13)
LOR	Law on Ownership Rights (OG of MNE, No. 19/09)
LP	Law on Public Procurement (OG of MNE, No. 42/11)
LP	Law on Political Parties (OG of MNE, Nos. 21/04, 73/10, 40/11, 59/11)
LPC	Law on Protection of Competition (OG of MNE, No. 44/12)
LPC	Law on Prohibition of Discrimination (OG of MNE, No. 18/2014)

List of Abbreviations

LPCI	Law on the Prevention of Conflict of Interests (OG of MNE, No. 01/09)
LPD	Law on the Protection of Personal Data (OG of MNE, Nos. 79/08 and 70/09)
LPIP	Law on Prevention of Illegal Businesses (OG of MNE, No. 29/13)
LPSB	Law on Public Services Broadcasting of Montenegro (OG of MNE, Nos. 79/08, 45/12, 054/16)
LPT	Law on Patents (OG of MNE, Nos. 66/08 and 49/11)
LPTIC	Law on Protection of Topographies of Integrated Circuits (OG of MNE, No. 75/10)
LT	Law on Trademarks (OG of MNE, No. 72/10)
LTJSC	Law on Takeover of Joint Stock Companies (OG of MNE, No. 18/11)
LTO	Law on Torts and Obligations (OG of MNE, No. 47/07)
ML	Media Law (OG of MNE, Nos. 82/08, 51/02, 362/02)
PC	Criminal Code (OG of MNE, No. 70/03, 13/04, 47/06, 40/08, 25/10, 32/11, 40/13, 56/13, 014/14, 042/15, 058/15)
RACC	Rulebooks on Audiovisual Commercial Communications (OG of MNE, No. 36/11)
RCDPS	Rulebooks on Conditions on Determining Programme Standards in Its Own Production (OG of MNE, No. 46/12…)
RPSEM	Rulebooks on Programme Standards in Electronic Media (OG of MNE, Nos. 46/10, 007/16)
RRPRPB	Resolution on Rules for Political Parties' Representation in Public Media Founded by State During the Election Campaign (OF of MNE, No. 4/98)
SAEL	Statute of the Agency for Electronic Media (OG of MNE, No. 46/10)

Other

ACC	Audiovisual Commercial Communications
AECPS	Agency for Electronic Communications and Postal Services
AEM	Agency for Electronic Media
AMSD	Directive 2010/13/EU of the European Parliament and of the Council DIRECTIVE 2010/13/EU OF THE EUROPEAN PARLIAMENT AND OF THE COUNCIL of 10 March 10, 2010 on the coordination of certain provisions laid down by law, regulation or administrative action in Member States concerning the provision of audiovisual media services (Audiovisual Media Services Directive)

List of Abbreviations

APPDAI	Agency for the Protection of Personal Data and Access to Information
CAOD	Convention on Access to Official Documents
EUROPEAN Convention	EUROPEAN Convention on Human Rights and Freedoms
FRY	Federal Republic of Yugoslavia
MNE	Montenegro
MSB	Media sSelf-rRegulatory bBody
OG	Official Gazette
PSB	Public Service Broadcasting
RTM	Radio and Television of Montenegro
SFRY	Socialist Federal Federative Republic of Yugoslavia
VRSJ	Vilnius Recommendations on Safety of Journalists

General Introduction

§1. General Background of The Country

1. Montenegro was recognized in the international arena as a sovereign nation on July 13, 1878 at the Peace Congress in Berlin.[1] After the First World War, the Kingdom of Montenegro ceased existence as a nation and was incorporated in the Kingdom of Yugoslavia. After the Second World War, Yugoslavia was transformed into a communist federation (Socialist Federative Republic of Yugoslavia—SFRY), and Montenegro became one of the six co-equal constituent republics of the SFRY. Montenegro did not regain its independence immediately after the break up of SFRY at the beginning of the 1990s, but opted to stay together with Serbia as part of Yugoslavia (Federal Republic of Yugoslavia—FRY) and consequently, after Serbian strongman Slobodan Milosevic was removed from power, in the loose union of Serbia and Montenegro. Its statehood was finally restored on May 21, 2006 after a referendum on independence held under the auspices of the European Union ("EU"). Montenegro subsequently became the 193rd member of the United Nations.

2. Today, Montenegro is an independent and sovereign state under a republican form of government. Article 1 of the Constitution states that Montenegro is a "civil, democratic, ecological, and the state of social justice is based on the rule of law." By signing the Stabilization and Association Agreement in 2007 with the European Communities and their Member States, the European integration process was formally initiated with Montenegro harmonizing its laws to that of the EU. Montenegro submitted its application for EU membership in December 2008.The European Council (EC) granted candidate country status to Montenegro in its December 2010 session. With regard to the NATO Alliance membership, the country joined the Partnership for Peace in 2006 and the Membership Action Plan in 2009. At present, Montenegro is at the doorstep of membership to NATO, waiting only for the ratification process to be finalized by the Member States. The country is also deeply involved in the accession talks for the EU membership.

3. Montenegro launched into intensified negotiations with NATO after the NATO Foreign Ministers' meeting in mid of 2014. NATO extended a formal invitation to Montenegro to join the Alliance in December 2015.Accession Protocol of Montenegro to NATO was signed in Brussels on May 19, with full agreement of all NATO members. The completion of all ongoing ratifications of the Accession Protocol of Montenegro to NATO is expected by mid-2017.

1. Darmanović, S., Politički *sistem Crne Gore u IZBORNI I PARTIJSKI SISTEM U CRNOJ GORI: Perspektiva razvoja unutarpartijske demokratije*, pp. 11–44. Constitution of Montenegro (OG of MNE, Nos. 01/07, 38/13).

4. Since regaining its statehood, Montenegro has become a member of multiple international organizations and institutions. Montenegro is a member of the United Nations and the Organization for Security and Cooperation in Europe. In January 2007, Montenegro became a member of the World Bank and the IMF. In December 2011, it became the 156th member of World Trade Organization. For the purpose of this work, it is relevant to mention that Montenegro is a member of the Council of Europe, so that all verdicts of the ECtHR are of strong relevance to its national legal system. As part of the state union of Serbia and Montenegro, by the end 2003, the country ratified the European Convention on Human Rights and Fundamental Freedoms and its protocols. After the split of its union with Serbia and upon resumption of its sovereign independence, Montenegro submitted a statement of succession to the Council of Europe in relation to all the conventions signed by the union. Thus, in May 2007, Montenegro became the 47th member of the Council of Europe. This meant that Montenegro has become part of the European Court of Human Rights ("ECtHR") legal system and obliged itself (Government and the Courts) to apply the ECtHR's decisions. The right to file a complaint with the ECtHR is guaranteed, according to the Article 34 of the European Convention on Human Rights and Fundamental Freedoms, to several legal entities. In fact, Montenegrin citizens, foreigners, stateless persons, business entities, and non-governmental organizations have the right to contest the decisions of national courts before this Court, in accordance with the European Convention on Human Rights and Freedoms (ECHR) for violations of rights prescribed by Convention.

I. Legal and Political System of the Country

5. The Constitution, the fundamental law of the land, declares Montenegro as an independent and sovereign state based on the rule of law. The Constitution provides supremacy of the international law in comparison to national statutes. Article 9 of the Montenegrin Constitution states that ratified and published international agreements and generally accepted rules of international law shall constitute an integral part of the internal legal order, shall have the supremacy over national legislation, and shall apply directly when they regulate relations differently than the national legislation. Furthermore, the rights and liberties in Montenegro are defined and shall be exercised based on the Constitution. The strongest legal act also provides for the limitations of the guaranteed human rights and freedoms, stating that only the law can limit rights, for the prescribed purposes, and within the scope permitted by the Constitution. It further stipulates that all laws and regulations need to comply with the Constitution.

6. It guarantees equality before the law, regardless of any particularity or personal feature, permanence, autonomy, and independence of judges of the courts, thus effectively separating this branch of authority and advancing its professional and non-political quality in order to make it a safeguard of democracy and the rule of law.[2] In accordance with the Constitution, the laws shall regulate different issues: (1) the manner of exercise of human rights and liberties, when this is necessary for their exercise; (2)

2. Darmanović, S., Politički *sistem Crne Gore u IZBORNI I PARTIJSKI SISTEM U CRNOJ GORI: Perspektiva razvoja unutarpartijske demokratije*, pp. 11–44.

the manner of exercise of the special minority rights; (3) the manner of establishment, organization, and competences of the authorities and the procedure before those authorities, if so required for their operation; (4) the system of local self-government; (5) other matters of interest for Montenegro.

7. Under its Constitution and as operationalized in its political arena, Montenegro is a parliamentary democracy with a multi-party system.[3] The basis of the Montenegrin political system is defined under the Part 3 of the Constitution. It declares and stipulates several globally recognized rights such as: electoral right, freedom of thought, conscience and religion, freedom of expression, objection of conscience, freedom of press, prohibition of censorship, access to information, freedom of assembly, freedom of association, prohibition of organizing, prohibition of operation and establishment, right to address international organization, right of recourse. The political rights are rooted in the electoral right. This right to elect and stand for elections is guaranteed to anyone who is 18 years old and above with at least a two-year residence in Montenegro. The electoral right shall be exercised in free and direct elections, by secret ballot.[4]

A. Powers of Executive, Legislative, and Judicial Branches of Government

8. The power is regulated and limited by the Constitution. Article 11 of the Constitution states that the division of the power is defined in accordance with the principle of the division of powers into the legislative, judicial, and executive, based on balance and mutual control, limited by the Constitution and the law. The President of Montenegro in the country and abroad, represents Montenegro. The Prime Minister heads the Government of Montenegro and exercises executive power; the Parliament of Montenegro exercises legislative power; and courts of general jurisdiction, commercial courts, and the Constitutional Court exercise judicial power.

1. The President of the Republic

9. The President represents Montenegro. The role and jurisdiction of the President is mainly regulated by two legal acts: the Constitution of Montenegro and Law on the Election of the President.[5] The President is elected for a period of five years, through direct and secret ballot. He cannot assume the duty for more than two times. Its mandate can end on four ways: (1) by expiration of the term; (2) by resignation; (3) by permanent incapability to perform the duty; and (4) by impeachment. The President enjoys the same extent of immunity as representatives in the Parliament (Article 98).

10. Impeachment of the President can be initiated if he or she violates any provision of the Constitution for which he can be held accountable. As stated in Article 98, the procedure may be initiated at the proposal of a minimum twenty-five members of Parliament. The Constitutional Court shall make the decision on the existence or

3. Darmanović, S., Politički *sistem Crne Gore u IZBORNI I PARTIJSKI SISTEM U CRNOJ GORI: Perspektiva razvoja unutarpartijske demokratije*, pp. 11–44.
4. Constitution of Montenegro (OG of MNE, Nos. 01/07, 38/13).
5. Constitution of Montenegro (OG of MNE, No. 01/07), Law on the Election of the President of Montenegro (OG of MNE, Nos. 17/07, 08/09).

nonexistence of the violation. After the Constitutional Court finds that the Constitution has been violated, the Parliament may impeach the President of Montenegro.[6]

11. The responsibilities of the President of Montenegro are provided under Article 95 of the Constitution. Article 95 states that the President represents Montenegro in the country and abroad, commands over the Army on the basis of the decisions of the Defense and Security Council, proclaims laws by Ordinance, calls for the elections for the Parliament, and proposes to the Parliament the following: a candidate for the Prime Minister, after consultations with the representatives of the political parties represented in the Parliament; President and judges of the Constitutional Court; and Protector of human rights and liberties. He also appoints and revokes ambassadors and heads of other diplomatic missions of Montenegro abroad, at the proposal of the Government and after obtaining the opinion of the Parliamentary Committee responsible for international relations, accepts letters of accreditation and revocation of foreign diplomats, awards medals and honors of Montenegro, grants amnesty, performs other tasks stipulated by the Constitution or law.[7]

2. The Government

12. The Prime Minister represents the Government of Montenegro. The Government consists of a Prime minister, one or several deputy prime ministers and ministers. The President's proposal for the Prime Minister initiates the election of the Prime Minister. The Parliament with the majority of vote of all members shall decide simultaneously on the Government program and the proposal for the composition of the Government.

13. The Government is accountable to the Parliament. The Government term ceases in three cases: (1) with the expiry of the Parliament mandate; (2) by resignation, when it loses confidence; and (3) if it fails to propose the Budget by March 31 of the budgetary year. The Government whose mandate has ceased shall continue with its work until the election of the new composition of the Government. Parliamentary control over the Government may be pursued with three instruments: (1) Issue of no-confidence; (2) Interpellation; and, (3) Parliamentary investigation. The Government may raise the issue of confidence before the Parliament. The proposal for a no-confidence ballot regarding the Government may be submitted by minimum twenty-seven Members of the Parliament. If the Government gained confidence, the signatories of the proposal shall not submit a new proposal for a no-confidence ballot prior to the expiry of the ninety days deadline. Resignation or dismissal of a Prime Minister entails the dismissal of the entire Government. In addition, the interpellation to examine certain issues regarding the work of the Government may be submitted by minimum twenty-seven Members of the Parliament. In fact, the same number of Parliament members may establish a Fact-finding Commission in order to collect information and facts about the events related to the work of the state authorities.

14. As stated in Article 100 of the Constitution, the Government has responsibility to: manage internal and foreign policy of Montenegro; enforce laws, other regulations and general acts; adopt decrees, decisions and other acts for the enforcement of laws;

6. Constitution of Montenegro (OG of MNE, No. 01/07).
7. Constitution of Montenegro (OG of MNE, No. 01/07).

sign international agreements; propose the development plan and spatial plan of Montenegro; propose the budget and the final Statement of the budget; propose the national security strategy and defense strategy. It also shall decide on the recognition of states and establishment of diplomatic and consular relations with other states; nominate ambassadors and heads of diplomatic missions of Montenegro abroad; and perform other tasks stipulated by the Constitution or the law.[8]

3. The Parliament

15. The legislative power is vested in a unicameral Parliament, consisting of eighty-one members. They are elected for a four-year term directly by the general electorate through secret ballot. The mandate of the parliament may cease prior to the expiry of that period by dissolving it or reducing the mandate of the Parliament. If the mandate of the Parliament expires during the state of war or the state of emergency, the mandate shall be extended up to three months.

16. The Parliament has a Speaker and one or more Deputy Speakers. The Speaker of the Parliament represents the Parliament and has the duty to: call for the sessions of the Parliament, take care of the enforcement of the Rules of Procedure of the Parliament, call for elections for the President of Montenegro and perform other affairs stipulated by the Constitution, as specified under Article 89 of the Constitution. The Deputy Speaker substitutes the Speaker whenever he is prevented to do so.[9]

17. The members of the Parliament have the right to propose laws and other acts, as stated in Article 93 of the Constitution. Six thousand voters are granted the right to propose laws through the Members of the Parliament. In addition to it, the proposal to call for a national referendum may be submitted by minimum of twenty-five deputies of the Parliament.

18. Members of the Parliament have immunity. As specified in Article 86, they cannot be held liable for expressing opinions nor be detained without the approval of the Parliament, unless they are caught committing a crime punishable by imprisonment of at least five years. The Parliament works in regular and ad hoc sessions. Regular sessions shall be held twice a year, whereas the extraordinary session shall be called for at the request of the President of Montenegro, the Government or a minimum of one-third of the total number of Members of the Parliament, as determined under Article 90. Parliament decides by majority vote of the present Members in the session attended by over one-half of the total number of Members, unless otherwise regulated by the Constitution. It decides by a two-third majority of the total number of the Members on the electoral system laws and property rights of foreign nationals.[10]

19. As provided under Article 82, the Parliament has jurisdiction over: the adoption of the Constitution; adoption of laws; adoption of other regulations and general acts (decisions, conclusions, resolutions, declarations, and recommendations); proclamation of the state of war and the state of emergency; adoption of the budget and the final statement of the budget; adoption of the National security strategy and Defense strategy; adoption of the Development plan and Spatial plan of Montenegro;

8. Constitution of Montenegro (OG of MNE, No. 01/07).
9. Constitution of Montenegro (OG of MNE, No. 01/07).
10. Constitution of Montenegro (OG of MNE, No. 01/07).

making decision on the use of units of the Army of Montenegro in the international forces; regulation of the state administration system; performing supervision of the army and security services; call for the national referendum; election and dismissal from duty the Prime Minister and members of the Government; election and dismissal from duty the President of the Supreme Court, the President and the judges of the Constitutional Court; appointment and dismissal from duty: the Supreme State Prosecutor and State Prosecutors, the Protector of human rights and liberties (Ombudsman), the Governor of the Central Bank and members of the Council of the Central Bank of Montenegro, the President and members of the Senate of the State Audit Institution, and other officials stipulated by the law; making decisions on immunity rights; granting amnesty; confirming international agreements; call for public loans and decide on borrowings of Montenegro; making decisions on the use of state property above the value stipulated by the law; performance of other duties stipulated by the Constitution or the law.[11]

4. Judiciary

20. In Article 188 of the Constitution, courts are autonomous and independent in their work. They shall rule on the basis of the Constitution, laws, confirmed and published international agreements. In the *civil law* countries, the judicial power is divided between the ordinary and constitutional judiciary. The ordinary judiciary in Montenegro is organized into three court systems. In accordance with the Article 14 of the Law on Court Organization, courts established in Montenegro are: Basic courts, Higher courts, and the Commercial Court.[12] The amendments to the Constitution of 2013 have ensured the functional independence of the courts in Montenegro. In fact, these amendments envisaged that Judicial Council conducts election of judges, including Chief Justice. The establishment of this body is composed of ten members who have the jurisdiction of electing and dismissing all judges in the country. This solution has been generated under the recommendation of the Venice Commission of the Council of Europe to contribute to the independence of the judiciary protecting it from the political influence.[13]

21. The organization of courts is regulated by Law on Courts Organization.[14] Article 8 of this text specifies the following court structure present in Montenegro:

(1) Misdemeanor Court;
(2) Higher misdemeanor Court;
(3) Basic courts;
(4) Higher courts;
(5) Commercial courts;

11. Constitution of Montenegro (OG of MNE, No. 01/07).
12. Law on Court Organization (OG of MNE, No. 39/11).
13. Screening Report Montenegro, Chapter 23 - Judiciary and Fundamental Rights, WP Enlargement + Countries Negotiating Accession to EU MD 281/12, 12.11.12, available at http://ec.europa.eu/enlargement/pdf/montenegro/screening_reports/20130218_screening_report_montenegro_ch23.pdf, pp. 3–4.
14. Law on Court Organization (OG of MNE, No. 39/11).

(6) Appellate Court of Montenegro;
(7) Administrative Court of Montenegro;
(8) Supreme Court of Montenegro.

22. As it can be seen from this division, there is a clear distinction between commercial courts and courts with civil jurisdiction. As stated in the Article 11 of the Constitution, constitutionality and legality are in the hands of the autonomous and independent Constitutional Court. The Constitutional Court has jurisdiction to determine the constitutionality of any law; legal questions and cases may be initiated by the court, other state authority, any local self-government authority, five Members of the Parliament, or by any other person. Under Article 150 of the Constitution and Article 19 of the Law on the Constitution Court any person may file an initiative to open the procedure for the assessment of constitutionality and legality. The Constitutional Court itself may also initiate the procedure for the assessment of constitutionality and legality. In the same article, Constitution states that the Constitutional Court may order to stop the enforcement of an individual act or actions that have been taken on the basis of the law, other regulation or general act, the constitutionality, i.e., legality of which is being assessed, if the enforcement thereof could cause irreparable damage.[15]

23. The amendments of 2013 have also regulated the election of the members of the Constitutional Court for a period of twelve years, by two-thirds majority in the Parliament. As provided under Article 149 of the Constitution, the Constitutional Court has jurisdiction on deciding on: (1) conformity of national laws and ratified international treaties with the Constitution; (2) conformity of all other legal acts with the Constitution and laws; (3) constitutional appeal due to the violation of human rights and liberties granted by the Constitution, after all other effective legal remedies have been exhausted; (4) whether the President of Montenegro has violated the Constitution; (5) the conflict of responsibilities between courts and other state authorities, between state authorities and local self-government authorities, and between the authorities of the local self-government units; (6) prohibition of work of a political party or a non-governmental organization; (7) electoral disputes and disputes related to the referendum, which are not the responsibility of other courts; (8) conformity with the Constitution of the measures and actions of state authorities taken during the state of war or the state of emergency; (9) performs other tasks stipulated by the Constitution.[16]

B. Political Parties

24. From 1990, Montenegro has adopted a multi-party system. In fact, since 1998 no single party could gain power alone, so that the country has been led by a coalition government consisting of two or several political parties. Montenegrin Constitution, in Article 53 states that political parties may be established freely, without prior approval, by the registration with the competent authority. Although the liberal political parties can be freely established, the Constitution prohibits all activities of

15. Constitution of Montenegro (OG of MNE, No. 01/07), Law on the Constitutional Court (OG of MNE, Nos. 64/08, 46/13, 51/13).
16. Constitution of Montenegro (OG of MNE, No. 01/07), Law on the Constitutional Court (OG of MNE, Nos. 64/08, 46/13, 51/13).

the political and other organizations directed toward forceful destruction of the constitutional order, infringement of the territorial integrity of Montenegro, violation of guaranteed freedoms and rights or instigating national, racial, religious, and other hatred and intolerance, as stated in Article 55 of the Constitution.[17]

25. The organization and functioning of the political parties are mainly regulated by the recent law on political parties, the law on financing of political subjects and electoral campaigning, and the law on amendments of electoral law,[18] which are harmonized with the European regulation, such as the Code of Good Practice in Electoral Matters and the OSCE Copenhagen Document.[19] Together with the NGO groups, political parties are the most active part of Montenegrin society. Only political parties, however, compete through the election process over political power.[20]

II. Geography and Population

A. Geography and Climate

26. Montenegro is a Mediterranean country of 13,812 km^2, located in Southeastern part of the Balkan Peninsula. The bordering countries are: Albania, Bosnia and Hercegovina, Croatia, Kosovo and Serbia. The capital and largest city is Podgorica whereas Cetinje represents the old royal capital and former seat of the monarchy. Podgorica has 185,937 inhabitants, while Niksic as former industrial city is the second largest city with 72,443 inhabitants.[21] Montenegro ranges from high mountains to a narrow coastal plain. Depending on the region, Montenegro has various kinds of different climates with strong differences and followed by the Montenegrin relief. There are three parts: Southern (coast), Central (continental), and Northern (the mountainous) regions.[22]

27. The Southern part contains the Coastal region. It has 293 km long coastline with 117 sandy and pebbly beaches. It is a narrow strip of land extending from Herceg-Novi to the Bojana river, on 73 km, with numerous creeks and bays, settled at the foothill of Mt. Orjen. The central or so-called continental part is urban and economically developed with the largest cities such as Podgorica, Cetinje, Danilovgrad, and Niksic.

17. Constitution of Montenegro (OG of MNE, No. 01/07), Law on the Constitutional Court (OG of MNE, Nos. 64/08, 46/13, 51/13).
18. Law on political parties (OG of MNE, Nos. 21/04, 73/10, 40/11, 59/11), Law on financing political subjects and electoral campaigning (OG of MNE, No. 52/14).
19. CODE OF GOOD PRACTICE Guidelines and Explanatory Report adopted by the Venice Commission, at its 52nd Session, Opinion No. 190/2002, CDL-AD (2002) 23 rev Or. Fr., available at whttp://www.venice.coe.int/webforms/documents/default.aspx?pdffile=CDL-AD(2002)023rev-e, Document of the Copenhagen Meeting of the Conference on the Human Dimension of the CSCE, available at http://www.osce.org/odihr/elections/14304?download=true.
20. Law on Amendments of Electoral Law (OG of MNE, Nos. 4/98, 05/98, 17/98, 14/00, 18/00, 09/01, 41/02, 46/02, 45/04, 48/06, 56/06, 46/11, 14/14, 47/14).
21. Results of the 2011 census are available at http://www.monstat.org/ (website of the National Bureau of Statistics or Monstat).
22. MIPA, Montenegro Country Report Edition 2015 available at: http://www.mipa.co.me/dcs/MIPA-Country-Report-2015-web.pdf.

This region has predominantly two parts: dinar area and valley part. Dinar area with the mountains of Orjen and Rumija, loom over the coast. Valley area includes the fertile valley of the river Zeta, Bjelopavlićka valley, and Niksic field. The northern region, in three small cities is dominantly preoccupied with farming, wood industries, and agriculture. Geographically, it is mostly covered by mountainous area permeated with a lot of meadows, pastures, fields, lakes, rivers Piva and Tara, and beautiful canyons. There are also two national parks: one protected under UNESCO — Durmitor mountain of Tara Canyon, and Biograd forest—a rainforest near Kolasin.

Table 1. United States Central Intelligence Agency, The World Factbook, Montenegro

Territory	13,812 km^2
Capital city	Podgorica
Location	Southeastern Europe
Geographic coordinates	42 30 N, 19 18 E
Climate	Mediterranean climate
Land boundaries	625 km
Border countries	Albania 172 km, Bosnia and Herzegovina 225 km, Croatia 25 km, Kosovo 79 km, Serbia 124 km
Arable land	12.45%

Source: available at: https://www.cia.gov/library/publications/the-world-factbook/geos/print/country/countrypdf_mj.pdf.

28. The Montenegrin climate is mainly considered as Mediterranean. According to the different geographic features of three regions, the climate in Montenegro is very diverse—coastal, continental, and mountainous climate zone. In general, under Köpen scale, Montenegro is indexed as a Bs climate, which refers to hot dry climate with more than 70% of the precipitation in the winter. The capital city has a *hot* Mediterranean subtropical climate, classified as Csa under Köpen scale. Montenegro has on average 180 bathing days. The coastal area has dry summers and mild winters. The average summer air temperature at the coast is 27.4°C, whereas the maximum sea temperature is 27.4°C. The mountainous climate is sub-alpine. It has snowy and cold winters with a maximum of 3°C and a minimum temperature of around -6°C. The summers in the mountains are moderate, with temperatures reaching 23°C and falling to 9°C.[23]

B. Population and Minorities

29. The minorities in Montenegro are strongly protected under current laws. The laws of Montenegro ensures adequate representation of ethnic minorities in public

23. MIPA, Montenegro Country Report Edition 2015 available at: http://www.mipa.co.me/dcs/MIPA-Country-Report-2015-web.pdf.

institutions, and provides measures for inclusive education in all minority languages, electoral and fair representation of minorities at all levels of the society, access to employment, health insurance, and social welfare and property rights. The preamble of Montenegrin Constitution of 2007 states that Montenegro stands for "free and equal citizens, persons belonging to nations and national minorities living in Montenegro: Montenegrins, Serbs, Bosnians, Albanians, Muslims, Croats and others." Accordingly, it prohibits forceful assimilation "of the persons belonging to the minority nations and other minority national communities" (Article 80).[24]

30. In addition, Article 79 of the Constitution stipulates that persons belonging to minority nations and other minority national communities shall be guaranteed the rights and liberties, which they can exercise individually or collectively with others, *inter alia*: the right to exercise, protect, develop and publicly express national, ethnic, cultural, and religious particularities; the right to choose, use and publicly post national symbols and to celebrate national holidays; the right to use their own language and alphabet in private, public, and official use; the right to education in their own language and alphabet in public institutions and the right to have included in the curricula their history and culture; the right to have local self-government authorities in areas with significant population; the right to establish educational, cultural, and religious associations, with the material support of the state; the right to write and use their own name and surname also in their own language and alphabet in the official documents; the right, in the areas with significant share in total population, to have traditional local terms, names of streets and settlements, as well as topographic signs written in the language of minority nations and other minority national communities; the right to authentic representation in the Parliament and in the assemblies of some local self-government units; the right to proportionate representation in public services, state authorities, and local self-government bodies; the right to information in their own language; the right to establish councils for the protection and improvement of special rights. Further protection has been ensured through adoption of the Law on Prohibition of Discrimination (2014), under the auspices of the Venice Commission.[25]

31. Despite strong legal protection and affirmative measures, discrimination against minorities is still present. National and international reports inform on the existence of certain groups, which still suffer from discrimination and social exclusion. In a survey conducted by the Centre for Democracy and Human Rights (CEDEM) in April 2010, close to 73% respondents said they believed that discrimination was mostly or highly present in Montenegro. The respondents also believed that employment, access to services provided by public authorities and education were the main fields in which discrimination occurred.[26]

32. The last national census in Montenegro conducted in 2011 shows that Montenegro has 620,029 citizens, A more recent World Bank report in 2014 conveys that the number has increased to 621,800. The same national census states that the main ethnic group is Montenegrins with 44.98% of the total population. Serbs are present with 28.73%, Bosniaks with 8.65%, Albanians with 4.91%, Muslims with

24. Constitution of Montenegro (OG of MNE, No. 01/07).
25. Law on Prohibition of Discrimination (OG of MNE, No. 18/2014).
26. The survey of 799 respondents covering all parts of Montenegro is available at http://www.cedem.me/fajlovi/attach_fajlovi/pdf/april2010-2010-4-19.pdf.

3.31%,[27] Croats with 0.97%, Roma with 1.01%, Egyptian with 0.33%, and others 7.11%. As obvious from the given facts, none of the ethnic groups in Montenegro forms an absolute majority.

Table 2 Ethnic Structure of Montenegro in 2011

		Bosniak		*Muslim*	*Roma*	*Croat*		*Others*
44.98		8.65	4.91	3.31	1.01	0.97	0.33	7.11

Source: Monstat (2011).

33. Roma, Ashkali, and Egyptians, so-called RAE, represent the ethnic group which is marginalized from society.[28] Research conducted by UNICEF and the Office of the United Nations High Commissioner for Refugees (UNHCR) in 2008 has conducted research showing widespread illiteracy and low education levels, jeopardizing their rights and ability to access basic services.[29]

34. Thirty percent of the total population—around 185,937 inhabitants—is concentrated in the country's largest city, Podgorica. The second biggest is Niksic with 72,443 inhabitants followed by Bijelo Polje with 46,051 inhabitants.[30]

III. Social and Cultural Values

35. The geographic location of Montenegro has conditioned its rich, and diverse history as well as the social and cultural influences of Ancient Rome, the Byzantine Empire, the Ottoman Empire, the Republic of Venice and Austria-Hungary. Montenegro is regionally recognized as a multi-faith and multi-ethnic society, committed to a formal policy of integration and equal rights. The highest Montenegrin legal act states that Montenegro shall encourage, support and protect the cultural, scientific, artistic, and historic values. In addition, it has strongly declared by Constitution the obligation to protect and preserve the national and cultural heritage of general interest.

27. In former Yugoslavia (SFRY), Muslims have been recognized as an ethnic group since 1981. After the dissolution of Yugoslavia, Muslims in Bosnia and Hercegovina decided to name themselves the ethnic group of "Bosniaks." The majority of Muslims in Serbia and Montenegro followed this decision. This was the reason why in the national census of 2001, "Bosniaks" for the first time appeared as an ethnic group, whereas a small minority still decided to keep the name Muslims. As a consequence, the census of 2011 in Montenegro presented two ethnic groups – Bosniaks and Muslims.
28. National Human Development Report 2009 Montenegro: Society for All (NHDR), United Nations Development Programme (UNDP) in Montenegro, 2009, available at *http://www.undp.org.me/home/actualities/NHDR.pdf*.
29. Civil Registration and the Prevention of Statelessness: A Survey of Roma, Ashkali, and Egyptians in Montenegro, United Nations High Commissioner Refugees – UNHCR and United Nations Children's Fund – UNICEF, May 2009. CEDEM, Mapping of the Anti-discrimination Legal, Institutional, and Policy Framework in Turkey and the Western Balkans. Country Report: Montenegro, p. 3.
30. MIPA, Montenegro Country Report 2011, p. 13 available at: http://www.mipa.co.me/userfiles/file/MIPA%20Country%20report%202011%20web.pdf, February 15, 2014.

36. The religious diversity of Montenegro is a consequence of the strong co-existence of three main religions: Orthodox, Catholicism, and Islam. According to the census of 2011, 72% of the population identify themselves as Orthodox (together Montenegrin and Serbian Orthodox Church), Muslims—followers of Islam religion—most of them belonging to the Sunni branch, amounts to 20% of the total population (118,447), whereas 3.4% of the population belongs to the Roman Catholic. In addition, the census of 2011 showed 350 Jews living in Montenegro. 1.25% of the population identify themselves as the atheists. Along with the three main religions, there are seventeen religious groups in Montenegro and some of them are: Adventists, Buddhists, Protestants, Jehovah's Witnesses, and Mormons.[31]

37. Article 13 of the Constitution of Montenegro declares Montenegrin language as the official language. Serbian, Bosniak, Albanian, and Croatian languages are declared by the same Article 13 to be "in official use." This Constitutional determination to have one official and several languages in official use, means that minorities may use one of these languages in administrative and court proceedings, when issuing public documents and keeping official records, preparing ballot papers, and other electoral material as well as in the work of representative bodies. In some parts of Montenegro with significant numbers of persons belonging to minority, the names of public bodies, the name of the local self-government unit, settlements, squares and streets, institutions, businesses and other entities, and topographical indications are written in the language and alphabet of that minority.

38. With an architectural heritage influenced by the baroque, gothic, and pre-Romanesque styles, cuisine influenced by Mediterranean, Turkish, and Hungarian tastes, and traditional dance influenced by Crmnicki Oro (epic Montenegrin songs with a one string instrument called the Gusle), Montenegro is regionally recognized as a country of pluralistic, diverse, and enriched cultural and social ambient.

§2. The Media Landscape

I. Overview of Media Markets and Main Actors

39. The Montenegrin economy is based on the principles of market economy, open and free market, freedom of entrepreneurship, independence of business entities and equality of private and other types of assets. Since the 1990s, Montenegro has been transitioning to a market system in all areas but, until recently, the state sector has remained at large. During the privatization of the economy and the transformation of the political system in Montenegro, the media sector has evolved under the principles of pluralism and prevention of monopoly. The development and proliferation of independent media outlets was encouraged by the end of 1990s, when international organizations urged their establishment.

40. The proliferation of various media outlets has been seen as an indicator of pluralism and endurance of Montenegro's media sector. In accordance with the European

31. Montenegro 2013 International Religious Freedom Report, available at: www.state.gov/documents/orhanization/222461.pdf, pp. 1–11.

integration agenda, Montenegro has repeatedly proved its determination to ensure the freedom of expression. Starting from 2002, when Montenegro abolished the penalty of imprisonment as a sanction for defamation, Montenegro has been acting in accordance with the European Council's recommendations. Thus, Montenegro reformed its laws and adopted legal texts in accordance with European legal standards on freedom of expression. The current legal framework, however, often does not ensure the adequate implementation.

41. The Montenegrin media sector has been recently recognized as rich one, with the present plurality of both print and electronic media outlets. In accordance with the statistics provided by Ministry of Culture and Agency of Electronic Media, there are 700 registered print media in Montenegro, of which only 50 are active. In the area of electronic media, there are 78 active electronic media, 22 television stations (2 channels with RTM, 3 local public TV channels, 17 commercial TV channels, out of which 4 with the national frequency) and 56 radio stations (40 commercial, 2 with RTM, 14 local public radio stations). Access to the internet is not restricted. In 2013 approximately 57% of the population had access to it, whereas in 2014 it was over 60%.[32]

42. The youngest media market—online media market—has developed rapidly in the last two decades. The widespread accessibility of the internet and the easy dissemination of the information posted online have potential long term effects on individuals. In Montenegro, the online media market itself is non-regulated. Under the LEM, the set up, functioning, and monitoring of online media has not been precisely defined. Although there are already several online media portals: Portal of public service www.RTM, Vijesti www.vijesti.com, Café del Montenegro www.cdm.com, Portalanalitika www.portalanalitika.me, Mina Agency www.mina-info.me, the rules defining their organizations have not yet been adopted. The Agency of Electronic Media has announced the adoption of such an instrument in the near future. In the current Law on Electronic Media they are named: ‚electronic publications," "editorially formatted web pages" or "portals that contain electronic versions of print media" and/ or "information from the media in a way that they are available to the general public regardless of their range."[33]

43. Publications and articles on the internet are "one of the most participatory form of mass speech yet developed" (*Reno v. American Civil Liberties Union*; *Delfi AS v. Estonia, ECtHR Judgment* (June 16, 2015) Application No. 64569/09; *Magyar*

---

32. Brkic, D., *Media Ownership and Financing in Montenegro: Weak Regulation Enforcement and Persistence of Media Control*, available at: http://www.mminstitute.org/files/Medijsko%20vlasnistvo%20i%20finansiranje%20medija%20u%20Crnoj%20Gori%20(1).pdf, pp. 7–9. Also *see* : Camovic, M., *Media Institut of Montenegro, Radno pravni status novinara u Crnoj Gori – NOVINARSTVO IZMEĐU STRAHA ZA EGZISTENCIJU*, Podgorica, 2015, available at: http://www.mminstitute.org/files/Izvjestaj%20radna%20prava%20MNE.pdf, Report of the Special Rapporteur on the promotion and protection of the right to freedom of opinion and expression; Frank La Rue, *United Nations General Assembly*, A/HRC/26/30/Add.1, Distr. General April 29, 2014, available at https://www.crin.org/sites/default/files/freedomofexpression_2.pdf, p. 13.

33. Brkic, D., *Media Ownership and Financing in Montenegro: Weak Regulation Enforcement and Persistence of Media Control*, available at: http://www.mminstitute.org/files/Medijsko%20vlasnistvo%20i%20finansiranje%20medija%20u%20Crnoj%20Gori%20(1).pdf, pp. 7.

Tartalomszolgáltatók Egyesülete and Index.hu Zrt v. Hungary (February 2, 2016) Application No. 22947/13). As globally noticed, its fast growth assumes "the unedited free-to-post user-generated-content sections." The user comments have generated the practice of hate speech and defamatory statements which were recently analyzed before the Court. In the famous internet case of *Delfi AS v. Estonia, ECtHR Judgment* (June 16, 2015) Application No. 64569/09, the Grand Chamber ultimately confirmed the Chamber's judgment and the ruling of Estonian courts, sanctioning the news portal for defamatory comments posted online by its readers. The Grand Chamber called upon "duties and responsibilities" of internet news portals when they provide for economic purposes a platform for users engaged in clearly unlawful speech which infringes on personality and reputational rights. The court found that the Directive on Electronic Commerce (2000/31/EC) did not apply to this case since it refers to merely technical, automatic, and passive activities, while Delfi's activities are more reflected to a huge professional internet news portal. Delfi's argument that it is a neutral intermediary and, therefore, immune from liability under the E-Commerce regime was rebutted by the argument that Delfi portal runs on a commercial basis, thus it should have exercised more caution in moderating comments. Delfi has a substantial degree of control over the comments published on its portal, so that it is liable for the readers' comments. In the case of *Magyar Tartalomszolgáltatók Egyesülete and Index. hu Zrt v. Hungary* (February 2, 2016) Application No. 22947/13, the ECtHR went further and determined the liability of a self-regulatory body of internet news portals (non- commercially-run Internet news portal) and content providers for vulgar and offensive online comments posted on their websites. This case definitely confirmed the previous findings on liability of the internet news portals for readers' comments broadening the range and scope of the actors.[34]

44. In the area of print media, according to the data available in Central Registry of the Tax Administration of 2016, there are four national Montenegrin daily papers. These are: Pobjeda, Dnevne novine, Vijesti i Dan. First two, in the national arena are seen as pro-government oriented, whereas Vijesti and Dan strongly advocating against government. Privatization of Pobjeda occurred ten years after stipulated timeframe. In fact, despite the 2002 Media law stringent provision that government must not have the majority stake which required the Government to sell its shares, Pobjeda as a state-owned newspaper with national circulation existed until November 2014.[35]

45. As of now, according to the Central Registry of the Tax Administration of 2015, Pobjeda is, 100% in the hands of Media Nea, LLC whose owner is Greek businessman Petros Statis. Dnevne novine, established in 2011, is owned 99.9% by Media Nea, LLC and 0.01% by Boris Darmanovic. These two daily papers are said to favor the government in its news coverage. According to unofficial data, the combined circulation of both dailies is around 10,000, with Dnevne novine delivering 6,000

34. Spaic, A., et al., *Decriminalization of Defamation - The Balkans Case a Temporary Remedy or a Long Term Solution?*, Int'l J.L., Crime & Just. (2016), http://dx.doi.org/10.1016/j.ijlcj.2016.05.002).
35. Brkic, D., *supra* ., pp. 7–9. Freedom of House Annual Report, 2014, https://freedomhouse.org/report/freedom-press/2014/montenegro#.VcwUuWCFPIU, Report of the Special Rapporteur on the promotion and protection of the right to freedom of opinion and expression, Frank La Rue, *United Nations General Assembly*, A/HRC/26/30/Add.1, Distr. General April 29, 2014, available at https://www.crin.org/sites/default/files/freedomofexpression_2.pdf, p. 11).

copies and Pobjeda less than 4,000, at the average price of 0.7 cents. In the same group of pro-government oriented media are several public channels: RTM, TV PINK M, and TV PRVA. These two are affiliates of Serbian channels that are parts of larger regional media groups. TV PINK M as a part of PINK Media Group in the possession of Zeljko Mitrovic, while TV PRVA is 100% in the possession of Antenna Group founded by the Greek capital. Both of them are said to be unfair competitors in the media market of Montenegro, due to their business strategy of low pay for advertising services in Montenegro. As stated by Camovic, as long as their real advertising services are in Serbia, their Montenegrin services can be provided for a significantly discounted rate or even for free.[36]

46. On the other side, Vijesti and Dan, founded in the late 1990s, are both independent media outlets and the strongest critics of the Government of Montenegro. They have dominant market positions based on their estimated circulation data. According to Brkic, their combined circulation is around 14,000, with Dan accounting for 8,000 and Vijesti accounting for 6,000. Vijesti is composed by three main actors: publishing company Daily Press—Zeljko Ivanovic, Katarina Perovic, Ljubisa Mitrovic (44.2%), Media Investment Fund, USA (30.7%), Austrian Sterya Medien (25%) and several minor shareholders. DAN has been established by Jumedia Mont, in the possession of Mladen Milutinovic and Dusko Jovanovic, the main editor in chief who was murdered in 2004. On the same side of the polarized media scene is TV Vijesti, which entered the market as the expansion of the Vijesti print media, in the possession of the MEDIA Development Investment Fund, USA (34%), Andrej Perovic (21%), Miro Perovic (20%), Slavoljub Scekic (11%), twelve minor stakeholders (14%).[37]

47. In the national and international arena, there is a variety of organizations monitoring the functioning of media outlets in Montenegro. As stipulated in majority of their reports, although Montenegrin legal texts are written in the European spirit, freedom of expression has not improved significantly. In fact, in the Reporters Without Borders' report for the period 2011–2012, Montenegro was ranked 107th out of 179 countries. Surprisingly, two years later, it has deteriorated in position by 6 posts; in

36. Camovic, M., *Media Institut of Montenegro, Radno pravni status novinara u Crnoj Gori—NOVINARSTVO IZMEĐU STRAHA ZA EGZISTENCIJU*, Podgorica, 2015, available at: http://www.mminstitute.org/files/Izvjestaj%20radna%20prava%20MNE.pdf, p. 5.

37. Brkic, D., *supra* ., p. 11, Camovic, M., *Media Institute of Montenegro, Radno pravni status novinara u Crnoj Gori – NOVINARSTVO IZMEĐU STRAHA ZA EGZISTENCIJU*, Podgorica, 2015, available at: http://www.mminstitute.org/files/Izvjestaj%20radna%20prava%20MNE.pdf, Report of the Special Rapporteur on the promotion and protection of the right to freedom of opinion and expression, Frank La Rue, *United Nations General Assembly*, A/HRC/26/30/Add.1, Distr. General April 29, 2014, available at https://www.crin.org/sites/default/files/freedomofexpression_2.pdf, p. 13. European Commission, Commission Staff of Working Document, Montenegro 2015 Report, Accompanying the document Communication From The Commission To The European Parliament, The European Economic And Social Committee, And The Committee Of The Regions, Eu Enlargement Strategy, Brussels, SWD (2015) 210 final) Research of Media Unions http://www.cdm.me/drustvo/crna-gora/istrazivanje-pokazalo-novinari-se-najvise-susrecu-sa-radom-na-crno, Canovic, M., *Media Institut of Montenegro, Radno pravni status novinara u Crnoj Gori – NOVINARSTVO IZMEĐU STRAHA ZA EGZISTENCIJU*, Podgorica, 2015, available at: http://www.mminstitute.org/files/Izvjestaj%20radna%20prava%20MNE.pdf.

2015 it as ranked as 114th out of 180 countries in the World (Reporters Without Borders, 2015).[38]

II. Broadcasting Infrastructure

48. The broadcasting infrastructure in Montenegro is predominantly regulated by the Law on Electronic Media. Monitoring, compliance with the regulations, establishment of broadcasting media, competitiveness, diversity of the market, licensing, and advertising are covered under the law. Along with the Law of the Electronic Media, Digital Broadcasting Law, Law on Public Services Broadcasting of Montenegro, the Law on Electronic Communication provides for the major requirements for operation, obstacles, and elements of a functioning broadcasting infrastructure.[39] The implementation of the laws on broadcasting in Montenegro has been delegated to an autonomous and independent entity, the Agency of the Electronic Media, and Agency of the Telecommunications and Postal Regulation.

49. Despite its geographic size and small population, Montenegro has a diverse media broadcasting scene. From data available in 2015, the broadcasting industry consists primarily of twenty-three television channels, six of which have national coverage, and fifty-six radio stations. In fact, all of them, under the Law on Electronic Media can be classified into two main categories of the broadcasters: private and public (state-run) broadcasters. In addition, there are several TV channels from neighboring countries available *via* cable. The functioning and organization of the public broadcasters are defined in the *lex specialis* Law on Public Broadcasting Service. The main national public broadcaster, namely the Radio–Television of Montenegro (RTM), operates with three television channels and two radio channels. The public broadcaster is governed by a Council of five members who are appointed by the Parliament for a period of five years.

50. Since public service was financed by the state budget for a relatively long period of time, it has suffered from lack of private financial investment, quality programs, and lack of unbiased and independent programs. In the past, it has adapted several financing models: self-finance through the users' fee, pre-paid subscriptions, and financing from the state budget (1.2% of the total budget). In July of 2016, the law on public broadcasting has determined that the amount of state financing is set at 0.3% of the gross national income.[40] On the other hand, private commercial broadcasters

38. Spaic, A., et al., *Decriminalization of Defamation - The Balkans Case a Temporary Remedy or a Long Term Solution?*, Int'l J. L., Crime & Just. (2016), http://dx.doi.org/10.1016/j.ijlcj.2016.05.002).
39. The Swedish Bar Association and the New York City Bar Association, Independent Legal Mission to Study Press Freedom in Montenegro, May 2013, available at: http://www2.nycbar.org/pdf/report/uploads/Montenegro.pdf, p. 10.
40. Law on Public Services Broadcasting of Montenegro (OG of MNE, Nos. 79/08, 45/12, 054/16).

are self-financed, and in the national arena there are three: TV Vijesti, TV Prva, and TV Pink.[41]

III. Technological and Economic Developments on the Media Markets

51. The Stabilization and Association Agreement between EU and Montenegro, signed in 2007 and effective in 2010, provides that Montenegro has the obligation to promote, to make modern services accessible, and to remove obstacles to the effective activities of electronic communications services and networks. It also addresses the need to generate an effective regulatory framework for audiovisual media services on its path to the EU.

52. Since 2007, Montenegro has promoted the liberalization of the electronic communications networks and services market through promulgating the Law on Electronic Communications, 2008. Further amendments to the law in 2013 and 2016 adopted the BEREC Regulation (EC) No. 1211/2009 and 2002 EU regulatory framework for electronic communications as the part of "2009 Telecom Package." The changes incorporated provisions on the "promotion of open market, competition and consumer interests—discrimination in the treatment of undertakings, and non-discrimination in the treatment of undertakings."[42]

53. Accordingly, the Digital Broadcasting Law and Digital Agenda for Europe, under the Ministry for Information Society and Telecommunications, and Montenegro has developed a National Strategy and Plan on its Information Society Development with a focus on five development issues. These information society components are: (1) sustainability, (2) community, (3) public administration, (4) economic development, and (5) development of the media and broadcasting market.[43]

54. The adoption of the Digital Broadcasting Law and Digital Switchover Strategy on Digital System implemented in accordance with the EU practice and policy (contained in Information of European Commission COM (2003) 541, Information of European Commission COM (2005) 204, followed by SEC (2005), Information of European Commission COM (2005) 46) had significant impact in the development of the Montenegrin broadcasting industry.[44] The conditions, methods, and the procedure of switchover from analog to digital broadcasting and other matters of importance for digital broadcasting are defined within these documents. The Digital Broadcasting Law, under Article 10 specifies the obligation of the country to provide conditions for

41. Law on The Swedish Bar Association and the New York City Bar Association, Independent Legal Mission to Study Press Freedom in Montenegro, May 2013, available at: http://www2.nycbar.org/pdf/report/uploads/Montenegro.pdf, p. 10.
42. Screening report Montenegro Chapter 10 – Information society and media, available at http://ec.europa.eu/enlargement/pdf/montenegro/screening_reports/screening_report_montenegro_ch10.pdf, p. 2.
43. Screening report Montenegro Chapter 10 – Information society and media, available at http://ec.europa.eu/enlargement/pdf/montenegro/screening_reports/screening_report_montenegro_ch10.pdf, p. 2.
44. Montenegrin broadcasting platform, available at: http://www.ardcg.org/en/index.php?option=com_content&task=view&id=18&Itemid=18).

digital broadcasting of signals of the national public broadcasting services of the Radio and Television of Montenegro (RTM) through: (1) development of the first network carried out for coverage of the entire territory of Montenegro, at least for 85% of the population of Montenegro; and (2) funds provided for coverage of the increased costs for electricity in the switchover period for the first network operator. The digital system, after several years of preparation, has been fully introduced in Montenegro on June 17, 2016. The Broadcasting Center has the status of the first multiplex operator and the first network operator, without conducting a tender procedure for allocation of radio frequencies. It assumed its obligation to cover 85% of population through first network.

55. Article 15 of the Digital Broadcasting Law provides that period of switchover from analog to digital broadcasting of television programs in Montenegro shall commence upon the effective date of the Plan for Allocation of Radio Frequencies for Digital Terrestrial Broadcasting and shall be completed until June 17, 2015. By that date, any approved entity shall terminate broadcasting of their television programs in analog technique. Under Article 13 of DBL, a period of simultaneous analog and digital program broadcasting for public broadcasting services and audiovisual media service providers that acquired the right to multiplex access, "shall start upon provision of technical conditions for digital broadcasting of programs from the same broadcasting site." Simultaneous existence of the analog and digital program broadcasting may last for maximum six months—up to the end of 2016. Audiovisual media service providers shall inform the public on the switchover period as well as on the termination of analog program broadcasting. Upon expiry of the period of simultaneous analog and digital program broadcasting from the same broadcasting site, an audiovisual media service provider shall terminate program broadcasting through analog systems from that location, as well as other broadcasting locations with overlapping service zone.

56. Furthermore, the National Strategy and Plan on its Information Society Development has stated the success rates and measures, so that broadband development shall achieve 25% broadband access by 2014 and 40% by 2016, with the intention of further expansion. Screening report from October 2012 stated that "the fixed broadband penetration rate per 100 inhabitants amounted to 13,9%, while large differences in take-up between municipalities existed. With regard to fast and ultrafast internet access, 34 % of homes are in reach of an DSL network, around 2% of homes connected with fibre and around 10% having fixed wireless or mobile wireless access." Montenegro estimates that only "21% of Internet subscribers have access to broadband networks with speeds exceeding 2Mbps." Under the Strategy Montenegro has also established the aim to reach a level of penetration of internet users of 75% by 2015, and 85% by 2016. The policy and its implementation is under the responsibility of the Ministry for Information Society and Telecommunications.[45]

45. Screening report Montenegro Chapter 10 – Information society and media, available at http://ec.europa.eu/enlargement/pdf/montenegro/screening_reports/screening_report_montenegro_ch10.pdf, p. 2, Report of the Special Rapporteur on the promotion and protection of the right to freedom of opinion and expression, Frank La Rue, *United Nations General Assembly*, A/HRC/26/30/Add.1, Distr. General April 29, 2014, available at https://www.crin.org/sites/default/files/freedomofexpression_2.pdf.

57. The switchover process has been guided and monitored by the Agency of Electronic Media and Agency of Telecommunications and Postal Regulations. The cessation of the analog TV system resulted in a reduction of broadcasters using the analog system. At the same time, the number of the electronic media outlets which broadcast via KDS/MMDS/DTH/IPTV platforms increased, so that Montenegro has achieved very high transition to these forums. In fact, it is 85% of the Montenegrin households which have opted for the use of the one of these platforms. The Government of Montenegro and Agency for Electronic Media (AEM) have donated over 14,000 of the units for special categories of the population such as elders, persons with disability, and persons with financial need.[46]

58. The transition into electronic digital system by household consumers has been relatively high. By 2015, the first national multiplex (MUX1) embraced and supported the programs of two public channels (TVCG1 and TVCG2) and three commercial broadcasters (TV Vijesti, TV Prva, and TV Pink). However, because of the increasing debts and high anticipated expenses for the accession to MUX1, in 2015, majority of local providers have been reluctant in adopting this platform. After the second public call, several local commercial and public broadcasters were similarly granted access, namely: TV Teuta (MUX UL L1), TV BOIN (MUX PG-DG L1), TV Sun (MUX BP L1), TV Glas Plava (MUX PL GS L1), TV Niksic (MUX NK–PZ L1), TV Budva (MUX BD L1), TV Pljevlja (MUX PV GS L1).[47]

59. According to the Report of the Agency of Electronic Media of February 2016, electronic communications improved, so that in the last two months the number of connections increased by almost 7% (11,648), whereas that number in the last six months increased by approximately 8% (13,245). The same report confirmed that four national broadcasters (TVCG, TV Vijesti, TV Prva, and TV Pink) have obtained the right to access the first national multiplex—MUX1. Access to the local multiplex has been obtained via different platforms (KDS/MMDS/DTH/IPTV) by several local broadcasters: TV Teuta (MUX UL L1), TV BOIN (MUX PG-DG L1), TV Sun (MUX BP L1), TV Glas Plava (MUX PL GS L1), TV Niksic (MUX NK–PZ L1), TV Budva (MUX BD L1), TV Pljevlja (MUX PV GS L1). As of date of issue of the Report 2016, the number of the connections have reached the number of 178,517.[48]

§3. Sources of Media Law

60. The Stabilization and Association Agreement signed on October 15, 2007 between the European Communities and their Member States, and Montenegro, has legal, political and economic conditions for the future development of Montenegro on its way to accession to the EU, in accordance with the principles of the rule of law, human and civic freedoms, and economic freedoms in Montenegro. As an international

46. Agency of Electronic Media, Annual Report of 2015, available at: http://www.ardcg.org/en/index2.php?option=com_docman&task=doc_view&gid=99&Itemid=4.
47. Agency of Electronic Media, Annual Report of 2015, available at: http://www.ardcg.org/index.php?option=com_docman&task=cat_view&gid=43&Itemid=26, p. 3.
48. Agency of Electronic Media, Annual Report of 2015, available at: http://www.ardcg.org/en/index2.php?option=com_docman&task=doc_view&gid=99&Itemid=4).

agreement, in accordance with Article 9 of the Constitution of Montenegro, the Stabilization Agreement prevails over the laws in Montenegro. It provides that Montenegro shall make a legislative effort to harmonize and make compatible EU with domestic laws. Furthermore, Montenegro shall ensure proper implementation of the adopted legal texts.[49]

61. As mentioned previously, the sources of media law are rooted in the international and national legal arena. The international component has been established via constitutional provision regarding the legal supremacy of the international provisions. In that context, Article 9 of the Constitution of Montenegro directly incorporates international agreements into domestic law by providing that "ratified and published international agreements and generally accepted rules of international law shall constitute an integral part of the internal legal order." It also states that "it shall have the supremacy over national legislation and shall be directly applicable when they regulate relations differently from national legislation." Article 145 further stipulates that domestic laws "shall be in conformity with the Constitution and confirmed international agreements, and other regulations shall be in conformity with the Constitution and the law." Direct determination of the application of the European law has been defined under the Media Law and Law on Electronic Media. Both legal texts explicitly proclaim the guarantee on freedom of information at the level of the standards as contained in the international documents on human rights and freedoms and also court practice of European Court of Human Rights.

62. Regarding the Constitution, there are specific provisions regulating four main feature-components of the freedom of speech regulation in Montenegro. These characteristics are specified under the Articles 47, 49, 50, 51. First, freedom of the press is defined and stipulated under the Article 49: "Freedom of press and other forms of public information shall be guaranteed. The right to establish newspapers and other public information media, without approval, by registration with the competent authority, shall be guaranteed." It further states that "The right to a response and the right to a correction of any untrue, incomplete or incorrectly conveyed information that violates a person's right or interest and the right to compensation of damage caused by the publication of untruthful data or information shall be guaranteed."[50]

63. In addition, Article 47 defines and guarantees freedom of expression, as well as other rights limiting the freedom of expression. It states that: "Everyone shall have the right to freedom of expression by speech, writing, picture or in some other manner. The right to freedom of expression may be limited only by the right of others to dignity, reputation and honour and if it threatens public morality or the security of Montenegro."[51]

64. Furthermore, Article 50 of the Constitution clearly prohibits censorship in the following manner: "There shall be no censorship in Montenegro. The competent court may prevent dissemination of information and ideas via the public media if required so as to: prevent invitation to forcible destruction of the constitutional order

49. Spaic, A., *Autonomy and Antidiscrimination in Private Law*, in *Civil Law Forum for South East Europe, Collection of Studies and Analyses Reich* (N., Jessel-Holst, C., Josipovic, T. eds., *Skopje, Deutsche Gesellschaft fur Technische Zusammenarbeit* 2014).

50. Constitution of Montenegro (OG of MNE, No. 01/07).

51. Constitution of Montenegro (OG of MNE, No. 01/07).

defined by the Constitution; preservation of territorial integrity of Montenegro; prevention of propagating war or incitement to violence or performance of criminal offences; prevention of propagating racial, national and religious hatred or discrimination." The Constitution under Article 51 provides for the content of the right to access information: "Everyone shall have the right to access information held by the State authorities and organizations exercising public authority. The right to access to information may be limited if this is in the interest of: the protection of life; public health; morality and privacy; carrying of criminal proceedings; security and defense of Montenegro; foreign, monetary and economic policy" (Article 51).[52]

65. National legal sources can be divided into direct and indirect legal text regulating the freedom of expression. Along with laws referring to media issues indirectly such as Criminal Law and Law on intellectual property, there are five legislative texts directly dealing with legal issues involving the media, namely: Media Law (2002), Law on Electronic Media (2012), Law on Public Broadcasting Services (2012), Law on Digital Broadcasting (2011), and Law on Free Access on Information (2012). Also, there are three other national laws that indirectly address issues that are relevant for the regulation of freedom of expression such as Criminal Code, Law on Liabilities of Legal Entities for Criminal Offenses, and Law on Intellectual Property.

66. The Media Law establishes general principles and solutions on which the media system in Montenegro is based. It declares media in Montenegro free, prohibits censorship and establishes that Montenegro shall provide and guarantee freedom of information at the level of the standards as contained in the international documents on human rights and freedoms and also court practice of European Court of Human Rights. The Law on Electronic Media regulates the process of licensing of the transmission and broadcasting of radio and television signals. It governs the rights, duties, and responsibilities of legal and natural persons pursuing the activities of production and provision of audiovisual media services. It also defines the status, competences, and financing for the AEM, as an independent regulatory body with the tasks of adopting the Broadcasting Development Strategy and Monitoring audiovisual broadcasters. It regulates the prevention of unlawful media concentration, promoting media pluralism. It further provides for the establishment of a public broadcaster—RTM. Law on Public Services Broadcasting stipulates the activities of Public service broadcasting (PSB)—RTM, as well as its financing scheme, organization and manner of work. It defines in detail the competences and functions of RTM Council and RTM Director General. Law on Free Access on Information defines the content of the Right on access to information held by public authorities—public bodies, public companies, and other entities performing public powers. It prescribes that the principles of free access to information, transparency in work of public authorities, the right of the public to know and equality of request. It determines that the access to information shall be carried out at the level of standards set out in ratified international agreements on human rights and freedoms and in general principles of international law. The Digital Broadcasting Law defines the instruments and procedural aspects for digital terrestrial broadcasting, including the procedure of switchover from analog to digital broadcasting.

67. The Criminal Code in Articles 178 and 179 describe two crimes regarding the curtailment of freedom of expression. Article 178 of the Criminal Code defines

52. Constitution of Montenegro (OG of MNE, No. 01/07).

infringement of freedom of speech and public appearance, specifying that anyone who denies or restricts freedom of speech or public appearance of another person in an unlawful manner, shall be sentenced to a fine or imprisonment not exceeding one year. It further states that if this act is committed by a person acting in an official capacity, during performance of his/her duties, that person shall be sentenced to imprisonment not exceeding three years. Also, Article 179 specifies the offense on preventing of printing and distribution of printed matters, and broadcasting. Anyone who prevents or disturbs, without permission: (1) printing, recording, sale or distribution of books, magazines, newspapers, audio and video cassettes or other printed or recorded matters; or (2) broadcasting of radio or TV programs, shall be sentenced to a fine or imprisonment not exceeding one year. If this crime is committed by a person acting in an official capacity, during performance of his/her duties, that person shall be sentenced to imprisonment not exceeding three years. In addition, the Criminal Code in Article 180 provides for the crime on prevention of publication of responses and rectifications. It states that anyone who, contrary to the final decision by a court of law, rejects or prevents to publicize a response or rectification of an incorrectly published information which violates someone's rights or interests, shall be sentenced to a fine or imprisonment not exceeding one year.[53]

68. The Law on Contracts and Torts is also very relevant regarding media issues. The main violations in media reporting are to be settled in civil proceedings with the civil sanctions so that three articles of Law on Contracts and Torts are of huge significance of understanding media rights. For example, in the Chapter named Violation of dignity and spreading untrue allegations, Article 151 states that whoever insults another person's honor, or whoever utters or conveys false statements concerning another person's past, knowledge, and ability, or concerning anything else of the kind, although being aware, or should have to be aware, that these are untrue, thus causing material damage to such person, shall be liable for damages. However, one shall not be liable for the loss caused when the false statement concerning another was made without knowing that it is not true, should he or the one acknowledging the statement have a serious interest in the matter. Article 206 of the Law on Contracts and Torts provides that in case of violation of an individual right, the court may order: that sentence—the correction be made public, or order that the tortfeasor take back the statement causing the violation, or order something else which would reach the purpose. The same Law, in Article 207, states that "offended reputation, honour, freedom or rights of personality, the court shall, after finding that the circumstances of the case and particularly the intensity of pains and fear, and their duration, provide a corresponding ground thereof – award equitable damages, independently of redressing the property damage, even if the latter is not awarded."[54]

69. In addition to the Constitution and several herein mentioned bylaws, there is a number of the rulebooks and decisions relevant to the media area, such as Rulebooks on Audiovisual Commercial Communications, Rulebooks on Program Standards in Electronic Media, Rulebooks on Conditions on Determining Program Standards in Its Own Production.

53. Criminal Code (OG of MNE, No. 70/03, 13/04, 47/06, 40/08, 25/10, 32/11, 40/13, 56/13).
54. Law on Torts and Obligations (OG of MNE, No. 47/07).

Part I. Freedom of Speech

70. Article 10 of the European Convention of Human Rights provides that freedom of expression constitutes one of the essential foundations of a democratic society and is one of the basic conditions for its progress. Montenegro formally became a signatory of this Convention in 2007, although it was a de facto member since 2003. Thus, in accordance with this European Convention, the media environment in Montenegro is defined under the provisions of its Constitution (Article 47—The Right on Information, Article 49—Freedom of Press, Article 50—Prohibition of the Censorship, Article 51—Right to Access Information), the Media Law, and the Law on Electronic Media. Along with the European Convention, Montenegro assumed the obligations stipulated in other international treaties protecting freedom of expression and promulgated by the United Nations, the Organization for Security and Co-operation in Europe (OSCE), the Council of Europe, and the EU. Montenegrin law further guarantees the press freedom based on: the freedom of expression; freedom of investigation, collection, dissemination, publicizing and receiving information; free access to all sources of information; protection of man's person and dignity and free flow of information.[55] The rights of media and freedom of the press are paramount concerns, not only in the transitioning countries, but also in democratic countries. Thus, the correct understanding and implementing of their content is of enormous significance.[56]

71. The exact scope, and limitations of these rights are not easy to delineate especially in the undeveloped legal climate and inexperienced civil courts. The rights of media and the press often conflict with other legal rights of individuals, such as right to dignity or privacy. When two rights of the same conventional nature and strength come into conflict, the courts and the legal community are tasked with providing a framework for resolution. However, in countries that only have recently recognized the right of free press, there is the problem that these rights will be practiced in excess or even abused to the detriment of other conflicting rights such as the individual's right to privacy.[57] In this context, Montenegrin public concern has increased over the treatment of, and legal responses to, dissemination of incorrect information that may harm the honor or reputation of a person (Article 19, 2003). In particular, two important issues are brought to the forefront when dealing with laws regarding freedom of expression: *first*, the right of an individual to protect himself or herself against false statements that damage his or her reputation; and, *second,* how to balance an individual's privacy rights without unduly restricting another individual's freedom of expression. Current Montenegrin legislation and court practice seek to achieve the balance of privacy rights with freedom of expression but it has been difficult to achieve. All countries shall have

55. Spaic, A., et al., *supra* ., p. 12.
56. Vodinelić, V., *Pravo masmedija*, Fakultet za poslovno pravo, Beograd, 2003, p. 16. Nikolić, D., *Medijsko pravo*, Službeni glasnik, Beograd, 2010. p. 71.
57. Spaic, A., et al., *supra*., p. 2.

legal standards and methods to determine this ratio, however, the form and content of their approaches differ widely, especially within the context of defamation laws.

72. With respect to the Montenegro's position regarding the violation of the Article 10 of the European Convention, ECtHR passed two judgments, which have strongly determined future practice of the national Montenegrin courts. These cases are: *Sabanovic v. Montenegro and Serbia, ECtHR Judgment* (May 31, 2011) Application No. 5995/06 and *Koprivica v. Montenegro, ECtHR Judgment* (November 22, 2011) Application No. 41158/09.

73. In *Sabanovic v. Montenegro and Serbia case, ECtHR Judgment* (May 31, 2011) Application No. 5995/06, Montenegrin daily newspaper published an article about the quality of the water in the Herceg-Novi area, calling upon the Institute for Health report. It has condemned the conduct of the Chief State Water Inspector. In this verdict "the ECHR stated that public has not only the right to information that is inoffensive, but also to those that offend, shock or disturb." The Court upheld the right to disseminate "information on matters of public interest even where the statements in question involved are untrue and damaging about private individuals, if claimed in good faith." In the case of *Koprivica v. Montenegro, ECtHR Judgment* (November 22, 2011) Application No. 41158/09), the editor Koprivica, defamed two officials of the International Criminal Tribunal for the former Yugoslavia (ICTY) by stating that they "prepared the file with sixteen names of the journalists in ex Yugoslavia who were to be tried for incitement." The ECtHR found that the award of damages consisting of twenty-five month pension of the applicant was excessively disproportionate.

74. Reports of the monitoring entities usually analyze the period before and after decriminalization of defamation. The Internal Report of MSS, 2014 states that in period of 2003–2010 there has been 117 cases, addressing 108 immaterial compensations and 7 material compensations. From 2010 to 2013, there have been 52 cases addressing 45 immaterial and 7 material compensations. Out of 52 cases for the period of three years, there were 27 cases against Dan, 20 against Vijesti and 5 against Monitor. The enhancement of the media environment can be accomplished only by strong commitment of all actors: academic society, lawyers, journalists but also of the lay public.

Part II. Regulation of Print Media

Chapter 1. The Journalists' Profession

75. The journalism profession has not been highly appreciated in Montenegro. Freedom House[58] underlines that political polarization of media actors in Montenegro often triggers failure of the professionalism of media. Consequently, the lack of professionalism among media practitioners and journalists contributes to further tensions on the media market. Montenegrin legislative framework does not provide the specific rules or conditions to be fulfilled in order to work as a journalist. In fact, there is a certain number of journalists working without a bachelor's degree in journalism or any other university degree, although there is no precise statistic on it.[59]

76. According to the 2013 Monstat static report, out of 174,156 employed people in Montenegro there are 1,972 journalists. OSCE Report on the journalists' unions of 2014 reports that there are 809 journalists in 57 media outlets in Montenegro.[60] Furthermore, Camovic states that a small advertising market and at the same time, a large number of broadcast and print outlets exacerbated three media bankruptcies (3 TV stations, 3 radio stations, 1 daily paper).[61] According to the Media Institute Report which called upon Union of Journalists' data, 500 journalists were left without jobs in a period of three years. As provided in by the Agency of Employment, in 2015, there were in total 112 unemployed journalists: 38 unemployed with a bachelor's diploma, 21 of the graduate level, and 29 graduates under the old education system, and 24 graduates for sports journalism.[62]

77. The main education provider for journalists in Montenegro is Faculty of Political Science and Faculty of Sport (for sport journalism) of University of Montenegro. The faculty is licensed for four education levels: bachelor, graduate, master, and

58. Freedom House is the non-governmental organization founded in 1941 with the purpose of defining each country's degree of democracy, civil liberties, political freedoms with the focus on monitoring violence and intimidation against journalists, censorship, and public access to information. *See* more at: https://freedomhouse.org/.

59. Freedom House, Nations in Transit 2012 – Montenegro, June 6, 2012, available at: https://freedomhouse.org/report/nations-transit/2012/montenegro.

60. Camovic, M., *Media Institut of Montenegro, Radnopravni status novinara u Crnoj Gori – NOVINARSTVO IZMEĐU STRAHA ZA EGZISTENCIJU*, Podgorica, 2015, available at: http://www.mminstitute.org/files/Izvjestaj%20radna%20prava%20MNE.pdf, p. 10.

61. Freedom House, Report 2014, available at: https://freedomhouse.org/report/freedom-press/2014/montenegro#.VcwUuWCFPIU.

62. Camovic, M., *supra.*, p. 11.

doctoral level. According to the official data 314 students have obtained bachelor, 189 graduate and 25 master level studies.[63]

78. Along with the category of the journalists with a regular contract and pay, Camovic reports on the freelancers and bloggers, who often assume journalist tasks, but are not treated accordingly. According to the 2015 Report of Media Institute of Montenegro, bloggers have neither been recognized nor defined in the Montenegrin legal regulation. In the interviews conducted for the purpose of writing the above-mentioned report, bloggers cannot live on the profit acquired through that activity. In fact, majority of them work for other standard media outlets. Thus, they do not have the status nor the capacity of a journalist.[64]

79. The journalism profession has significantly weakened. Monitoring reports on media allude to and at the same time express concern about the growing number of violence and threats against media outlets and journalists reporting on corruption, organized crimes, and government officials' business and political affairs.[65] Under the auspices of UN Special Reporter, Montenegrin Government has formed the Committee for investigating violence and threats against the journalists and media, consisting of the government, media, and NGOs. The Commission for monitoring the activities of the competent authorities in the investigation of old and recent cases of threats and violence against journalists was set up in December 2014. It included representatives from the Ministry of Interior, the prosecutor's office, the police, the National Security Agency, NGOs, and media representatives. As of fall 2016, it had neither found strong evidence nor rendered conclusive results; thus, the public has consequently concluded a lack of accountability, and that impunity for those crimes could encourage additional attacks.

80. The Montenegrin judiciary, to a certain extent, has been successful in resolving some cases involving violence against journalists and attacks on media property. However, in others, investigations are pending and there are no concrete results. On the contrary, "both the material perpetrators and those allegedly behind the attacks remain to be identified." The most important cases which have attracted the attention of the national and international community for different reasons are the following: Case of Dusko Jovanovic (2004), Case of Lidija Nikcevic (2014), Case of Andrej Nikolaidis (2007), Case of Zeljko Ivanovic (2007/2010), Case of Mladen

---

63. Camovic, M., *supra* ., p. 8.
64. Camovic, M., *supra.* , p. 6.
65. Camovic, M., *Media Institut of Montenegro, Radnopravni status novinara u Crnoj Gori* – NOVINARSTVO IZMEĐU STRAHA ZA EGZISTENCIJU, Podgorica, 2015, available at: http://www.mminstitute.org/files/Izvjestaj%20radna%20prava%20MNE.pdf, p. 10, Freedom House, Nations in Transit 2012 – Montenegro, Jun. 6, 2012, available at: https://freedomhouse.org/report/nations-transit/2012/montenegro. Network for Affirmation of NGO Sector (MANS), "How much does it cost for a journalist to be critical in Montenegro?", p. 5, available at: http://www.mans.co.me/en/wp-content/uploads/fai/FreedomOfExpression-Internship.pdf, Report of the Special Rapporteur on the promotion and protection of the right to freedom of opinion and expression, Frank La Rue, *United Nations General Assembly*, A/HRC/26/30/Add.1, Distr. General Apr. 29, 2014, available at https://www.crin.org/sites/default/files/freedomofexpression_2.pdf, Brkic, D., *Media Ownership and Financing in Montenegro: Weak Regulation Enforcement and Persistence of Media Control*, available at: http://www.mminstitute.org/files/Medijsko%20vlasnistvo%20i%20finansiranje%20medija%20u%20Crnoj%20Gori%20(1).pdf).

Stojovic (2008), Case of Mihailo Jovovic (2009), Case of Petar Komnenic (2011), Case of Olivera Lakic (2012), and Case of Veselin Drljevic (2012). These cases are of different nature, depending on the subject of violation. In fact, in case of Olivera Lakic, the journalist was physically attacked, whereas in the case of Andrej Nikolaidis, the question raised was on the amount of damages found by the courts. In the extreme case of Dusko Jovanovic, the journalist was murdered, and as for now, the case has not yet been resolved.[66] Thus, violence against journalists remains a source of serious concern.

66. Network for Affirmation of NGO Sector (MANS), "How much does it cost for a journalist to be critical in Montenegro?", p. 5, available at: http://www.mans.co.me/en/wp-content/uploads/fai/FreedomOfExpression-Internship.pdf.

Chapter 2. Journalists' Rights

§1. Role of Journalists As Watch-Dogs of Society

81. As globally accepted and confirmed "democracy watchdogs"—journalists are required to be sharp observers of all social, political, and economic processes. They function as the keepers of established democracies as well as the reformers of the transitional systems. Their integrity and their professional attitude toward public and public interest, impartiality and professionalism, standard of due diligence shall be a guarantee for the professionalism of the media actors. However, Montenegrin reality is somewhat different.

82. If their actions are perceived to be manipulated by political actors or for economic gain, and their reports are viewed unethical or the result of political calculation, their role in society as promoters of democracy comes into question. Thus, it is necessary to determine effective remedies against malpractice, unethical and unprofessional reporting and ask *Quis custodiet ipsos custodes?*[67]

83. Under current Montenegrin laws that decriminalized defamation, when a journalist damages another person's reputation, honor, or dignity there is no other liability except for monetary compensation or fine. There is no criminal charge, but only civil procedure aimed at an award of damages. The latest proposal in Media Law limits this amount to up to four Montenegrin average salaries or less than EUR 2,000, in accordance with the known rule *In maxima potentia minima licencia.*[68]

84. The duties of journalists are defined under the Codex of Montenegrin Journalists, 2016 written under the auspices of OECD. Under the general principle that a journalist serves the public interest and that his profession shall rest on professional honesty, integrity, and knowledge, a journalist is obliged to defend freedom and has the right to collect and announce information without being disturbed. Journalist shall respect the truth and persistently search for it, having in mind a right of the public on the concise and timely information. Thus, the facts should be sacred for a journalist, and it is his duty to put them in the right context and prevent their misuse. They shall be immune from anything that can limit or bring into suspicion his autonomy and impartiality, and affect his or her ability to make decisions. Rumors and assumptions should be clearly marked as such. It is a duty of a journalist to complete the incomplete

67. Spaić, A., *Media Coverage in Minor Proceeding: In the Light of Krone Case of ECHR* (Krone case), Godina VII Broj 13–14, Podgorica November 2012, ISSN 1800-7074 COBISS.CG - ID 12734480, available at: https://medijskidijalozi.files.wordpress.com/2013/02/md-broj-13-14.pdf. Resolution on journalistic freedoms and human rights, adopted at the 4th European Ministerial Conference on Mass Policy (Prague, Dec. 7–8, 1994) and Resolution European Parliament on the confidentiality of journalists' sources January 18, 1994, OJEC No C 44/34.

68. For further discussion on the relationship between moral and legal norms *see* , for instance: Ossowska, Maria *Moral and Legal Norms*, 57 The J. of Phil. 7, 251–258 (1960).

and to correct the incorrect information, especially one that can cause harm, and at the same time to make sure that the correction is pointed out in an adequate manner.[69]

§2. Journalists' Independence

85. By definition, the freedom of expression is the strongest pillar of democracy and engine of the democratic process. On its European path, Montenegro has set the principles of pluralism and declared freedom of expression in Montenegro. Journalists shall exercise fundamental rights and freedoms, including the right of free speech, in accordance with the legal standards, ethics, and other principles of professionalism. However, these key principles of professionalism and impartiality are often questioned. The freedom and responsibility shall be linked. Having a strong voice shall generate accountability for deliberately reporting falsehoods in order to accomplish its role in accordance with a moral and legal code of ethics. Unfortunately, freedom of expression by insulting and belittling another has nothing to do with either democracy or freedom. Generally speaking, reporting in Montenegro is portrayed as a combination of sensationalism and political ambition.[70] In fact, it is often difficult to determine whether unethical reporting is a consequence of lucrative and/or political ambitions or just the result of pure ignorance. Journalists are not highly paid, and in the conjunction with the lack of knowledge and political interference, they often do not produce quality work, but biased coverage. In addition, intimidation of and violence against journalists as well as attacks on media property have curtailed media freedom and the democratic climate.[71]

86. The majority of monitoring entities have agreed on the low level of the freedom of expression in Montenegro. Media outlets' polarized political division and reporting, influenced either by the government or strong business interests, often cannot be trusted. Political polarization and lack of professionalism have been seen as the main features of the media outlets. These reports also state that the journalist profession can be essentially improved once the following diagnosed problems are resolved: (1) lack of strong professional support in the form of a solely self-regulatory journalist council; (2) diminishing the violence and intimidation against journalists and media outlets; (3) low pay; (4) lack of knowledge and training; (5) exposure to strong political and business influence. These problematic issues are correlated and mutually dependent.[72]

---

69. Journalists' Code of Ethics of 2016, available at http://www.osce.org/fom/255576?download=true.
70. Network for Affirmation of NGO Sector (MANS), "How much does it cost for a journalist to be critical in Montenegro?", p. 5, available at: http://www.mans.co.me/en/wp-content/uploads/fai/FreedomOfExpression-Internship.pdf., Nolasco, C., Spaic A., *Cenzura kao odgovor na (ne) etičko izvještavanje medija, ZBORNIK – Vjerodostojnost medija – nedostižan san, Montenegrin Academy of Science and Art*, ISBN 978-86-7215-389-7, pp. 39–51, January, 2017.
71. Spaic, A., et al., *supra* ., p. 12.
72. Freedom House, Nations in Transit 2012 - Montenegro, June 6, 2012, available at: https://freedomhouse.org/report/nations-transit/2012/montenegro, Freedom House, Nations in Transit 2014 - Montenegro https://freedomhouse.org/report/freedom-press/2014/montenegro#.VcwUuWCFPIU "Network for Affirmation of NGO Sector (MANS), "How much does it cost for a journalist to be critical in Montenegro?", p. 5, available at: http://www.mans.co.me/en/wp-content/uploads/fai/FreedomOfExpression-Internship.pdf.

87. In order to create independent journalists, they have to be properly paid. Regarding the issue of the journalists' salary, OSCE report states that the average journalist pay is less than an average pay in Montenegro (EUR 476 in September 2015). The monthly salaries vary depending on the media outlets but also on the positions or departments within the same media house. Although, there is no official data regarding this issue, Media Institute Report provides that highest paid actor in media is the main editor (around EUR 1,000) whereas the lowest paid actor gets around EUR 250. In same report, Media Institute of Montenegro stipulates that journalists are usually not paid for overtime or overload. They also encounter the problems of not having holiday/free days, delay in pays, and pays in installments. It is often reported that employers don't pay for the state contribution funds—for retirement, health, and social insurance. Furthermore, Camovic states that these are systematic and not sole examples of how media outlets mistreat their employees. They cannot complain about infringement of their rights, because they are threatened with being fired. To prevent this infringement, it has to be detected, and acknowledged by competent authorities. The state authorities are, however, very much hesitant to cope with these journalists' problems due to the potential harmful interpretations. In fact, state activities, even legal and legitimate ones, limiting or constraining the activities of the media outlets, will have political connotation and will have negative impact of Montenegrin external relations as well as its European integration aim. This refers especially to the media outlets who stand for major critic of the Government. In fact, although they lead in debt, all independent private broadcasters are in major debt to tax administration and the state agencies. These are the reasons why these serious journalists' problems remain unresolved to day.[73]

§3. Protection of Journalistic Sources

88. There are several regional legislative models regarding the issue of the protection of journalistic source. Whereas, for example, Serbian media law stipulates that journalistic sources can be disclosed if information relates to the crime sanctioned with five years of prison.[74] Montenegrin Medial law delineates that a journalist and other persons who, in the course of gathering, editing, or publicizing program contents, obtain information that could indicate the identity of the source, shall not be obliged to disclose to the legislative, judiciary, or executive authority or any other natural or legal person the source of information that wants to remain unknown.

89. According to the Recommendation No. R (2000) 7 of the Committee of Ministers to Member States on the right of journalists not to disclose their sources of information, the principles set in the Appendix of this text have to be properly disseminated to the journalists, the media and their professional organizations, public authorities, police authorities, and the judiciary and to ensure their implementation in

73. Camovic, M., *Media Institute of Montenegro, Radno pravni status novinara u Crnoj Gori – NOVINARSTVO IZMEĐU STRAHA ZA EGZISTENCIJU*, Podgorica, 2015, available at: http://www.mminstitute.org/files/Izvjestaj%20radna%20prava%20MNE.pdf, p. 9.

74. Law on media (OG of RS, Nos. 83/*2014*, 58/2015 i 12/2016), available at http://www.parlament.gov.rs/upload/archive/files/cir/pdf/zakoni/2014/2511-14.pdf.

the domestic law and practice the principles, in the members of the Council of Europe, where Montenegro belongs.[75]

90. Montenegro has, in several legal texts, enshrined the need for democratic societies to secure adequate means of promoting the development of free, independent, and pluralist media. The protection of journalists and their sources, however, have been established in its legal system only as the general principle, without further elaborating on meaning of the principle itself. Although stating that protection of journalists' sources of information constitutes a basic condition for journalistic work and freedom as well as for the freedom of the media, Montenegrin legal texts do not provide for the particular aspects of the journalists rights, duties, and responsibilities. On the contrary, Croatian Media Law has included all provision of the Recommendation No. R (2000) 7 of the Committee of Ministers.

91. The Appendix of the Recommendation (2000) 7 strongly advocates, *via* seven principles, the adoption of the domestic law and practice in order to provide for explicit and clear protection of the right of journalists and other persons who are in the professional relations with the journalists, not to disclose information identifying a source. However, Montenegrin law has not further specified the content of these seven principles: right of non-disclosure of other persons, limits to the right of non-disclosure, alternative evidence to journalists' sources, conditions concerning disclosures, interception of communication, surveillance and judicial search and seizure, protection against self-incrimination. These principles set in the Appendix of the R (2000) 7, as such need further implementation in the national legal texts. Given its sensitive nature, mere declaration on the right of the journalist not to disclose information identifying a source is not sufficient to adequately protect journalists.

75. Recommendation No. R (2000) 7 adopted by the Committee of Ministers on March 8, 2000 at the 701st meeting of the Ministers' Deputies.

Chapter 3. Journalists' Liability

§1. General Information on Liability System

92. Journalists are given a certain leeway to ensure freedom of the press and expression. As watchdogs of democracy, they have almost unbridled rights to criticize and publicize perceived wrongdoings of public figures. They are, however, expected to exercise their rights and duties determined in laws and Codex. Every single right within a democracy has its limits both moral and legal. Freedom and responsibility are linked, so that media must learn to bear the consequences of its crucial role in society. Journalists and media, with its strong voice, must be held accountable for deliberately reporting falsehoods in order to accomplish its role in accordance with a moral and legal code of ethics.[76]

93. The journalists' liability has been predominantly determined by the process of decriminalization of defamation. The process was initiated in 2003 when Montenegro abolished the prison sentence for defamation. Resolution 1577 (2007) of the Parliamentary Assembly of the Council of Europe on decriminalization of defamation calls on the Member States to "abolish prison sentences for defamation without delay," although, European Court of Human Rights has never explicitly stated that imprisonment is prohibited. The European integration process imposed on the EU candidate countries this obligation, whereas the vast majority of EU members does not have that standard. The Council of Europe required all potential Member States, among them Montenegro, to abolish criminal defamation laws and replace them with civil defamation laws.[77] The Special Rapporteurs of the UN (the OAS) advocated for the abolition of criminal acts of defamation by stating that criminal defamation is not a justifiable restriction on freedom of expression and that all criminal defamation laws should be replaced with civil laws. Also, domestic NGOs and media urged Montenegro to decriminalize defamation, arguing that criminal defamation has a "chilling effect" that may deter media or journalist from expressing his or her attitudes and feelings out of fear of a criminal litigation and sanction.[78] These actors painted the picture of societies that use the criminal law for this purpose as totalitarian and oppressive. Under these influences, in 2011, Montenegro has decriminalized defamation and has removed it from the Criminal Code of Montenegro.

94. Under current Montenegrin law, redress on these grounds can only be sought in civil procedures. Also, regarding previous cases of persons convicted of the criminal

76. Spaic, A., et al., *supra.*, p. 21.
77. Hulin, A., *Joint Declarations of the Representatives of Intergovernmental Bodies to Protect Free Media and Expression*. OSCE the Representative on Freedom of the Media. Vienna, 29. http://www.osce.org/fom/99558?download=true, 2013. p. 29; MANS, *supra.*, p. 1;), Resolution 1577 (2007) of the Parliamentary Assembly of the Council of Europe.
78. Barendt, E. et al., *Libel and the Media: The Chilling Effect*. Clarendon Press, Oxford, 1997.

offenses of insult and libel in Montenegro, Law on Amnesty of Persons Convicted of Insult and Libel was adopted.[79]

§2. Journalists' Special Liability Regime: The Liability of Journalists and/or Publisher

95. Freedom of expression is intrinsically linked to, not only legal, but also the moral liability of the media outlets and journalists for their wrongdoings. There are several legal texts in Montenegro specifying the civil and criminal liability of the journalists and media outlets. In the first place it has been directly regulated by Criminal Code (27–30), Media Law (Articles 20–26), and Law on Contracts and Torts. Criminal liability of the journalists is specified under the Criminal Code of Montenegro. The criminal liability for criminal offenses committed via media is stipulated in the Criminal Code of Montenegro, under the "Special provisions regarding criminal liability for criminal offences committed through the public information." In fact, Articles 28–30 define the liability of the editor in chief or their substitute, publisher, type-setter, and manufacturer.

96. The criminal liability of an editor in chief or the person who was on his/her position at the time when the information was published, if three conditions are met: (a) content was published without author's approval; (b) by the end of the first instance hearing, author is unknown; and (c) factual or legal impediments prevent the author's prosecution. (Article 28) When these conditions are met, law defines the liability of publisher, type-setter, and manufacturer. Publisher is held liable for a criminal offense committed through regular press publications. However, if publisher does not exist or there are actual or legal obstacles for his/her prosecution, the liable person is type-setter who was aware of it. When criminal offense is committed through some other instruments such as compact disc, phonograph record, magnetic tape and other audio means, film for public or private display, slides, videos or other similar means of communication intended for wider audience manufacturer, someone has to be criminally liable. In the situation that these persons are legal entities, liability will be borne by the person responsible for these activities (Article 29).

97. Founder of the media shall be accountable for every published programming. If a media published the programming that violates legally protected interest of a person, or that insults the honor or integrity of individual, gives or conveys untrue statements about his life, knowledge and abilities, or insults his dignity in any other way, the person interested shall have the right to press legal charges with the competent court against the author and founder of the media for the compensation of damage. (Article 20 of ML) It also states that "any information gathered in an illegal manner shall be published only in the interest of national security, protection of territorial integrity or public safety, prevention of disorder or criminal and health or moral protection, as well as the protection of reputation or rights of others, prevention of credential information disclosure or with the aim to protect the authority and impartiality

79. Spaic, A., et al., *supra* ., p. 12. *See Law on Amnesty of Persons Convicted of Insult and Libel* (OF of ME, No. 31/12), available at http://www.podaci.net/_gCGO/propis/Zakon_o_amnestiji/Z-alokdu04v1231.html.

of the judiciary" (Article 21 of ML). Furthermore, the Law provides that journalists shall not be held accountable if, in the course of their work, they obtain or publish the information that is considered to be state, military, official, or business secret, if there is an overriding interest of the public to be informed.

98. With regard to the prohibited contents, Media law defines that it is forbidden to publicize information and opinions that instigate discrimination, hatred, or violence against persons or group of persons based on their belonging or not belonging to a certain race, religion, nation, ethnic group, sex or sexual orientation. However, it states the situation when that founder of the media and the author shall not be held accountable. In fact, if the informative part of a scientific or authorial work, the subject of which is a public issue and is publicized: without intention to instigate discrimination, hatred or violence, especially if that information is a part of an objective news report; with intention to critically indicate the discrimination, hatred or violence or any phenomena which represent or might represent instigation to such behavior, the journalist will not be accountable (Articles 23–24 of ML).

99. Also, Law on Contracts and Torts provides for the cease of the activities of the media outlets which violate the individual rights. In this regard, Obligation Law specifies that everyone shall be "entitled to claim that the court or other competent agency order the cessation of an action by which the integrity of a human person, their personal and family life and other rights pertaining to their person are violated, as well as the reputation of a legal entity" (Article 151). It further underlines that the court or the other competent agency may order cessation of the action by threatening with an order to pay a certain amount of money, determined as a lump sum or per time-unit, to the benefit of the person suffering damage. Law on Contracts and Torts provides that in case of violation of an individual right, the court may order: that sentence—the correction be made public, or order that the tortfeasor take back the statement causing the violation, or order something else which would reach the purpose (Article 206). However, it further states that no one will be liable for the loss caused, when the one who makes the false statement concerning another did not know that it is not true, should they, or the one acknowledging the statement, have a serious interest in the matter. In the case of offended reputation, honor, or any other personal rights, the court shall, after finding that the circumstances of the case, such as intensity and duration of pains and fear provided, award equitable damages, independently of redressing the property damage, even if the latter is not awarded (Articles 151, 206, 207 of LCT).

§3. Defamation and Libel

100. The scope and content of freedom of expression can be analyzed through examining its impact and conflict with another important right—right to reputation. The right to reputation "has a much longer history" than right to freedom of expression—"reputation has been highly prized and strongly protected for centuries."[80] That also has been true for Montenegro. In cases where these two rights conflict, the court usually balances the impact, consequences, and significance of these two countervailing rights.

80. Barendt, E. et al., *Media Law: Text, Cases and Materials, Pearson Education Limited*, Harlow, England, 2014.

The purpose of this balancing test is to evaluate the gravity of the damage caused to someone's reputation against the value or relevance of the speech. Different national legal systems have different understanding of the criteria and reasons for strengthening or weakening the position of one or the other competing rights (reputation/speech). Accordingly, the ECtHR's intention is to provide a guideline for courts on how to balance freedom of expression and the right to reputation correctly, the balancing test—relevant principles. *First,* greater protection to ordinary subjects than special subjects of defamation (politician, public figure); *second* greater protection to value judgments than factual allegations; and, *third,* assessing the general purpose of defamatory statements.[81] The balancing test was created to draw the line between constitutional and conventional rights and to clarify specific issues, namely: (1) the necessity of limiting freedom of expression; (2) the proportionality of the limitation; and, (3) legitimacy of the limitation on the freedom of speech.[82] For example, one of the oldest cases *Sunday Times v. The United Kingdom, ECtHR Judgment* (April 26, 1979) Application No. 6538/74, contains one of the first and most important rulings of the ECtHR on freedom of expression. Here, the ECtHR allowed the publication of a newspaper article that discussed the public interest issues arising from, and the responsibilities of a drug company for, deformities of newborns caused by a drug manufactured by that company. In another *Bladet Tromso and Stensaas v. Norway, ECtHR Judgment* (May 22, 1999) Application No. 21980/93, the ECtHR concluded that "although the press must not overstep certain bounds, its duty is nevertheless to impart information and ideas on all matters of public interest." Thus, the Court held that freedom of expression and acting in good faith to provide accurate and reliable information is more important than the right to reputation.

101. Montenegro as an EU aspiring country has committed itself to gradually adjust its national legislation with the *acquis*, in accordance with Stabilization and Association Agreement and the European Partnership priorities, 2007. As stated, international community led by Council of Europe has urged Montenegro to decriminalized defamation. This process has to be seen as the part of harmonization with the EU laws, but also as the expression of more demanding legislative and practical standards posted on transitional countries. In the light of this request and in order to understand it, it is necessary to analyze the issues through the lens of EU practices and positions.[83] Namely, these requests demonstrate the double standards imposed on aspiring EU Balkan countries, and Montenegro as such. In discussions among members of the academic, society, and government, strong arguments have been advanced from both sides: those arguing for decriminalization of defamation and those arguing for its continued criminalization. Even if we recognize the necessity of decriminalization of defamation, we might still want to know why a democratic society might prefer to adhere to the "criminal" approach. In fact, the vast majority of the EU members have criminal defamation laws with imprisonment as a sanction. Some have laws where the punishment for defaming a public figure is harsher than the punishment for defaming an ordinary person. In contrast, Montenegro as transitional country is being requested to require a higher tolerance from politicians and other public figures that have been defamed.

81. Spaic, A., et al., *supra* ., p.12. Barendt, E., *supra* ., pp. 222–225.
82. Vodinelic, V., *supra.* , pp. 28–30.
83. MANS, *supra.* , p. 3.

Their argument is based on the fact that imperfect democracies need to understand that media's duty in a modern democracy is to enhance public debate without fear of reprisals in the criminal courts.[84] For example, regarding this issues, there is an ECHR judgment against Montenegro—the case of *Sabanovic v. Montenegro and Serbia, ECtHR Judgment* (May 31, 2011) Application No. 5995/06. Here, a Montenegrin daily newspaper published an article about the quality of the water in the Herceg-Novi area, stating that the current water sources contained various bacteria. The article was based on the Institute for Health report which had criticizing the conduct of the Chief State Water Inspector. The Chief Inspector filed a suit, claiming that the article's statements were untrue and harmful to his reputation. As the ECHR stated that public has not only the right to information that is inoffensive, but also to information that may offend, shock, or disturb. The Court has also already upheld the right to impart, in good faith, information on matters of public interest even where the statements in question involved are untrue and damaging statements about private individuals. The Court noted that the final criminal judgment at issue obviously amounted to an interference with the applicant's right to freedom of expression. The applicant had the right to criticize the Chief Inspector, because it referred to his official duties; thus, there was a violation of Article 10 of the Convention. Defamation of the public figure is one of the most important issues in defamation laws and jurisprudence. Majority of the court cases in Montenegro addressed the conflict between media's (and journalist's) freedom of expression and a public figure/politician's right to reputation (and dignity). The principles of the European Court of Human Rights, mandating greater protection for the media when writing about politicians had tremendous power in generating current national court practice. The Court invoked this reasoning in several cases to support its ruling that politicians must demonstrate a greater tolerance vis-à-vis statements directed against them by the public, including critical statements directed against them by the media (*Lingens v. Austria, ECtHR Judgment* (July 8, 1986) Application No. 9815/82; *Lopes Gomes da Silva v. Portugal, ECtHR Judgment* (September 28, 2000) Application No. 37698/97; *Oberschlick v. Austria (No. 2), ECtHR Judgment* (July 1, 1997) Application No. 20834/92; *Oberschlick v. Austria, ECtHR Judgment* (May 23, 1985) Application No. 11662/85; *Mladina v. Slovenia, ECtHR Judgment* (April 17, 2014) Application No. 20981/10; *Morar v. Romania, ECtHR Judgment* (July 7, 2015) Application No. 25217/06).

102. On the other hand the authors stating that criminalized defamation is the only proper response to defamation have posed several questions/dilemmas: (1) should media/journalists be held accountable for defamatory statements or libel through other means than the threat of damages in the form of money compensations; (2) to what extent can ruined reputation, honor, dignity be compensated by monetary damages only;[85] (3) the type of legal protection that should be given to an individual's reputation;[86] and (4) the contribution of decriminalization of defamation to the increase of media freedom or improvement of democratic conditions.[87]

---

84. Spaic, A., et al., *supra* ., p. 22.
85. Ossowska, M., *Moral and Legal Norms*. 57 The J. of Phil., 251–259 (1960).
86. Johnston, D., *The General Influence of Roman Institutions of State and Public Law*. http://iuscivile.com/legacy/reprints/j-1.pdf, 1997.
87. Spaic, A., et al., *supra.* , p. 14.

103. Along with the decriminalization, the second problematic issue raised is the determination of sanctions stated by the court once infringement is found. In fact, the same chilling effect on media reporting is detected in the award of high damage amount. In that context, the total amount of money paid in Montenegro up to 2013 reached up to EUR 1.7 million. The fines levied by Montenegrin courts are still, occasionally, high. In fact, in several documented cases journalists who wrote articles on problematic privatization deals covered by corruption, involvement of the government officials in organized crimes, war crimes, and other relevant and irrelevant issues have been sued on the bases of defamation. Several international reports pointed out that the overall amount of money paid on the ground for compensation reached up to EUR 1.7 million. They also specify that, by 2013, there were fifty-two cases against daily or weekly newspapers: "30 complaints pending against the daily newspaper *Dan*, with claims amounting to over 1 million Euros; 23 complaints amounting to almost 2 million Euros against *Vijesti*, and 9 cases against the weekly newspaper *Monitor*, amounting to 200,000 euros."[88]

104. In the case of (*Koprivica v. Montenegro, ECtHR Judgment* (November 22, 2011) Application No. 41158/09), the editor Koprivica, named two officials of the International Criminal Tribunal for the former Yugoslavia (ICTY) court who prepared the file with sixteen names of the journalists in ex Yugoslavia who were to be tried for incitement. Based on the ICTY's statement, the national court found that there was a violation of freedom of expression and ordered him to pay EUR 5,000 damages and EUR 2,677 for the legal costs. At that period, applicant's month pension was around EUR 130. The ECtHR found that the award of damages consisted of twenty-five month pensions of the applicant and was excessively disproportionate. This decision of the ECtHR was later used as reference by the Montenegrin Constitutional Court while reviewing a previous sentence of the Supreme Court. *Koprivica v. Montenegro* (application No. 41158/09).[89]

105. Contemporary Montenegrin law does not specify the formula to calculate the amount of damages. However, there are four legal grounds which are to be followed in the national arena:

106. First, The Declaration on freedom of political debate in the media, adopted in 2004 by the Committee of Ministers of the Council of Europe: Remedies against violations by the media: "Damages and fines for defamation or insult must bear a reasonable relationship of proportionality to the violation of the rights or reputation of others, taking into consideration any possible effective and adequate voluntary remedies that have been granted by the media and accepted by the persons concerned."

---

88. MANS, *supra* ., p. 12. United Nations Special Rapporteur on the right to freedom of opinion and expression, the OSCE Representative on Freedom of the Media, the Organization of American States (OAS) Special Rapporteur for Freedom of Expression and the African Commission on Human and Peoples' Rights (ACHPR) Special Rapporteur on Freedom of Expression and Access to Information, Tenth anniversary joint declaration: ten key challenges to freedom of expression in the next decade (2010), Spaic, A., et al., *supra.* , p. 12.

89. Report of the Special Rapporteur on the promotion and protection of the right to freedom of opinion and expression, Frank La Rue, *United Nations General Assembly*, A/HRC/26/30/Add.1, Distr. General April 29, 2014, available at https://www.crin.org/sites/default/files/freedomofexpression_2.pdf, p., Spaic, A., et al., *supra* ., p. 13.

107. Second, In addition, the rulings of the European Court of Human Rights have repeatedly stated that penalties for defamation and insult must be strictly limited and proportionate. The intention of European Court of Human Rights is to lower the award of damages.[90] In fact, the awards by the Strasbourg Court "are generally quite low" and that "recognition of the violation itself" is as an "efficient and exhaustive satisfaction for the victim, in many cases appearing to consider compensation as something merely added to such recognition."[91] In addition, the ECtHR has stated that disproportionate awards of damages in defamation cases can violate the right to freedom of expression. In particular, there are four interrelated concerns: the relevant issue is the determination of the amount of damages once infringement is decided. The ECtHR has stated that disproportionate awards of damages in defamation cases can violate the right to freedom of expression. In particular, there are four interrelated concerns: (1) the penalties for defamation and insult must be strictly limited and proportional to the damage caused; thus, there should be proportionality between the damage done by the defamatory remarks and the damages awarded; (2) the court must pay attention to the impact of the award on the journalist or media outlet concerned; (3) the court must have regard for the "chilling effect" of the damage award on the media in total; and, (4) the ECtHR requires clearly stated rules within the national legal systems. On this issue, the following rulings of the European Court of Human Rights have to be considered: *Barfod v. Denmark, ECtHR Judgement* (February 22, 1989) Application No. 11508/85; *Castells v. Spain, ECtHR Judgement* (April 13, 1992), Application No. 11798/85; *Şener v. Turkey, ECtHR Judgement,* (July 18, 2000), Application No. 26680/95; *Pakdemirli v. Turkey, ECtHR Judgement* (February 22, 2005), Application No. 35839/97; *Tolstoy Miloslavsky v. United Kingdom, ECtHR Judgement* (July 13, 1995), Application No. 18139/91; *Maronek v. Slovakia, ECtHR Judgement* (April 19, 2001), Application No. 32686/96). Even when in majority of these cases where the court found that the media violated someone's right to dignity and its writing was defamatory, the ECtHR has held that disproportionate awards of damages in defamation cases violate the right to freedom of expression (*Tolstoy Miloslavsky v. United Kingdom, ECtHR Judgement* (July 13, 1995), Application No. 18139/91; *Steel and Morris v. the United Kingdom, ECtHR Judgment* (May 15, 2005) Application No. 68416/01; *Koprivica v. Montenegro, ECtHR Judgment* (November 22, 2011) Application No. 41158/09; *Filipovic v. Serbia, ECtHR Judgment* (November 20, 2007) Application No. 27935/05; *Morar v. Romania, ECtHR Judgment* (July 7, 2015) Application No. 25217/06. In the case of *Tolstoy Miloslavsky v. United Kingdom, ECtHR Judgment* (July 13, 1995), Application No. 18139/91, for example, the ECtHR stated that, "[n] nevertheless, a disproportionately large award of damages (of 1.5 million pounds sterling) was found to be a violation of the rights guaranteed to the applicant under Article 10 of the European Convention on Human Rights" and that there were "lack of adequate and effective safeguards at the relevant time against a disproportionately

90. Spaic, A., et al., *supra* ., p. 13. OSCE. OSCE welcomes Montenegro's decriminalization of speech offences, available at: http://www.osce.org/montenegro/80808, 2013, p. 13.

91. Bona, M., *Towards The "Europeanization" Of Personal Injury Compensation: Contexts, Tools, Projects, Materials And Cases On Personal Injury Approximation in Europe,* in *Personal Injury Compensation in Europe*, (eds Bona M., Mead, P., Kluwer, Deventer, 2003). Spaic, A., et al., *supra* ., p. 11.

large award." Also, in *Morar v. Romania, ECtHR Judgment* (July 7, 2015) Application No. 25217/06, the ECtHR held that the amount of damages (more than fifty times the amount of the average wage at the time) was very high. In some of the cases however, the Court found the award of damages proportional to the injury caused by the defamatory statements (*Krone Verlag GmbH v. Austria, ECtHR Judgment* (June 19, 2012) Application No. 27306/07; *Independent News and Media and Independent Newspapers v. Ireland, ECtHR Judgment* (June 16, 2005) Application No. 55120/00, *Delfi AS v. Estonia, ECtHR Judgment* (June 16, 2015) Application No. 64569/09.

108. Third, Supreme Court Principal Legal Position establishes that pecuniary compensation for liability in defamation cases should be limited in accordance with the European standards defined by European Court of Human Rights and that the amount should not discourage journalists in their ethical conduct. Regarding this issue on determining the indemnity damages there is the Supreme Court Opinion on this question. If the Court finds the liability of journalists and media for false reporting—for the violation of personality rights (reputation, honor, etc.,) in order to determine the amount of damages the court has to take into account all the circumstances of the case. In particular: the importance of the injured goods and consequences as a consequence, the duration of mental hardship, to the aim it serves non-pecuniary damages, as well as the fact that the amount of compensation awarded as a rule, should be in accordance with the European Court of Human rights, and that it is not awarded compensation in the amount that would be discouraging or impose influence on journalists and the media in performing their role in the preservation of democratic values in society. However, the Supreme Court has not limited in advance the amount of non-pecuniary damage suffered. They found that that statement would be contrary to the principle of proportionality, as a fundamental principle of European law.[92]

109. Fourth, The Law on Contracts and Torts in the Article 151 states that whoever insults another person's honor, or whoever utters or conveys false statements concerning another person's past, knowledge, and ability, or concerning anything else of the kind, although being aware, or should have been aware, that these are untrue, thus causing material damage to such person, shall be liable for damages. However, one shall not be liable for the loss caused who makes the false statement concerning another without knowing that it is not true, should he or the one acknowledging the statement have a serious interest in the matter. Article 206 of the Obligations Act provides that in case of violation of an individual right, the court may order that, at the expense of the tortfeasor, the sentence, namely the correction, be made public, or it may order that the tortfeasor take back the statement causing the violation, or order something else which would reach the purpose, otherwise apt to be achieved by indemnity. However it further states that no one will be liable for the loss caused when the one who makes the false statement concerning another did not know that it is not true, should they, or the one acknowledging the statement, have a serious interest in the matter. Our legislature states that "offended reputation, honour, freedom or rights of personality, the court shall, after finding that the circumstances of the case and particularly the intensity of pains and fear, and their duration, provide a corresponding

92. The Supreme Court Opinion on this question published in the Bulletin 2011, The Supreme Court of Montenegro, ISNN 1800-5810.

ground thereof—award equitable damages, independently of redressing the property damage, even if the latter is not awarded."[93]

110. Decriminalizing defamation and libel has not promoted freedom of speech nor increased other democratic safeguards of speech in Montenegro. Although Montenegro decriminalized its defamation law, this decriminalization has helped neither the journalists nor the country in their efforts to democratize. Although the Montenegrin legal framework has abolished imprisonment as a sanction for libel, problems continue to exist in implementation. In fact, the courts "continue to award disproportionately high damages against journalists and media outlets in cases of libel."[94] A society that wants to ensure free speech must carefully balance the reputation rights of individuals against the freedom of speech of its citizens. This balance can be achieved through a wide array of instruments, including promoting freedom of expression among its citizens and the media, prohibiting undue censorship, and other civil safeguards such as damages and fines for transgressions of privacy without penal sanctions of imprisonment.

111. Article 20 of Media Law specifies that the media founder of the medium shall be accountable for programming which insults the honor or integrity of an individual, gives or conveys untrue statements about their life, knowledge and abilities, or insults their dignity in any other way. The person concerned shall have the right to press legal charges with the competent court against the author and founder of the medium for the compensation of damage. The Article 26 of the same legal text provides that a person whose constitutional rights have been violated in the broadcasted program is entitled to a right to reply, free of charge. The amount of fair compensation for damages due to the violation of personal rights (reputation, honor, and other personal rights) should be determined taking into account several reasons: the importance of the injured goods and the consequences of the injured goods, the duration of mental hardship and the aim of the damages. It means that awarded compensation should not have the discouraging impact on journalists and the media in performing their role in the preservation of democratic values in society. Thus, under current Montenegrin legal system, the cumulating of sanctions is permissible—if the injured party is not satisfied with the effect of the right of reply, the injured party is entitled to financial compensation in accordance with the Law on Contracts and Torts.[95]

§4. Privacy

112. One of the cornerstones of a democratic society is the right to privacy. With respect to the conventional strength, the freedom of expression is of equal significance to the freedom of the right to privacy, which assumes the respect for private and family life: "Everyone has the right to respect for his private and family life, his home and his correspondence. There shall be no interference by a public authority with the exercise of this right except such as is in accordance with the law

93. Spaic, A. et al., *supra* ., p. 11.
94. Spaic, A. et.al., *supra* ., p. 11.
95. OSCE. OSCE welcomes Montenegro's decriminalization of speech offences, 2011. http://www.osce.org/montenegro/80808, p. 13, Spaic, A., et.al, *supra.*, p. 11.

and is necessary in a democratic society in the interests of national security, public safety or the economic well-being of the country, for the prevention of disorder or crime, for the protection of health or morals, or for the protection of the rights and freedoms of others."[96] The exact content and boundaries of this right cannot be easily delineated due to its strong conventional character and nature.

113. Under Article 40 of the Constitution of Montenegro, the right of privacy is guaranteed. It states that "everybody shall have the right to respect for her/his right to private and family life." Article 42 of the Constitution of Montenegro provides for confidentiality of correspondence. In fact, it states that "confidentiality of letters, telephone conversations and other means of communication shall be inviolable." The principle of inviolability of confidentiality of letters, telephone calls and other means of communication shall be deviated on the basis of a court decision, if so required for the purposes of conducting criminal proceedings or for the security of Montenegro. Also, Article 43 provides guarantees for the protection of personal data. It is prohibited to use personal data for purposes other than those for which they were collected. Everyone shall have the right to be informed about the personal data collected about him or her and about the right to court protection in case of abuse.

114. The Law on Media is silent regarding the privacy right and media freedom of expression. Other than stating that the broadcaster is obliged to respect the privacy of the citizens, the Law on Electronic Media does not provide more. However, the Rulebook on the Programme Standards in Electronic Media provides detailed protection regarding this issue (Articles 12–16). This portion of the Rulebook states that the electronic media programmers shall not violate the privacy of individuals by publishing information concerning their private life, without their knowledge and consent, except in case of an overriding public interest. "Every violation of privacy shall be justified only in the case of an overriding public interest, especially when minors and people that are not public figures or are not in the public spotlight, are in question. When the programmers include statements concerning the improper activities or incompetence, or contain negative connotations concerning a certain person or organization, the people whose names have been mentioned shall be provided an opportunity to participate in the program and comment on these statements."

115. In electronic media programs that contain violent scenes and natural catastrophes, the media are bound by professional and ethical standards of journalists' code of conduct to appropriately inform the public, "express compassion, and eliminate any risk of sensationalism." Furthermore, "in reports on accidents or family tragedies, the right of victims or other affected persons to privacy must be respected" (Article 13). Also, if program broadcasting contains "data on persons, accidents, violence, mental consequences of violence," the electronic media shall respect the privacy of the survivors and/or family of the victims.

116. In addition to it, vulnerable persons and minors who cannot take care of themselves "shall not be interviewed about private matters without a written consent of their parents or guardians, except in cases when a difficult position of minors or vulnerable persons is discussed, for the purpose of encouraging the public to provide support." In fact, Article 14 states that the identity and personal data of minors or

---

96. Article 8 of the European Convention on Human Rights at: http://www.echr.coe.int/nr/rdonlyres/d5cc24a7-dc13-4318-b457-5c9014916d7a/0/englishanglais.pdf.

vulnerable persons shall not be revealed, in case there is a justified reason to believe that their publication could jeopardize their interest or dignity. Furthermore, it states that "the images of minors with developmental impairments shall not be used for any purpose that is not in compliance with the observance of their rights and human dignity. Consent is not necessary for the broadcasting of video materials showing anonymous members of public, in wide shots, without the possibility of clear identification and unrelated to any controversial topic, if it is clear that they have not been filmed on purpose. If random passers-by are filmed and interviewed on the street during the surveys, hidden camera shows, the material can be broadcast only if they provide their consent."

117. Montenegrin Criminal Code criminalizes five separate acts that infringe upon the right to privacy: infringement of privacy of mail and other means of communications (Article 172), unauthorized wiretapping and recording (Article 173), unauthorized photographing (Article 174), unauthorized publication and presentation of a somebody else's written texts, portraits, and recordings (Article 175), and unauthorized collection of personal data (Article 176). Infringement of privacy of mail and other means of communications exist when somebody without authorization opens someone else's letter, telegram, or other closed correspondence or means of communications or infringes in any other manner their inviolability or who withholds, conceals, destroys, or delivers to another person somebody else's letter, telegram, or other means of communications or who infringes privacy of electronic mail. Also, the same crime will exist when a person communicates to another the contents he has come to the knowledge of by infringement of privacy of somebody else's letter, telegram, or other closed correspondence or other means of communications or who makes use of such contents. For these conducts the prescribed sentence is a fine or imprisonment not exceeding one year. If these crimes are committed by a person acting in an official capacity, during performance of his/her duties, that person shall be sentenced to imprisonment not exceeding three years. One of the prohibited conducts often deployed by media is unauthorized wiretapping and recording. This crime exists when unauthorized taps by special listening devices or by recording a conversation, statement or any other information not intended for his/her use, or by a person who enables an unknown person to be informed about these materials shall be sentenced to a fine or imprisonment not exceeding one year. In addition to that crime, media, and journalists often resort to unauthorized photographing. In fact the Criminal Code in Article 174 provides that anyone who makes a photographic, film, video, or other recording of someone and thereby considerably violates the privacy of his life or who delivers or shows such recordings to a third party or enables a third party to come to the knowledge of such recordings, shall be sentenced to a fine or imprisonment not exceeding one year. If that person happened to be acting in an official capacity, during performance of his/her duties, that person shall be sentenced to imprisonment not exceeding three years. The unauthorized publication and presentation of a somebody else's written texts, portraits, and recordings is crime prescribed by Article 175. It states that anyone who publishes or publicly presents a written text, a portrait, a photograph, a film, or a phonogram of a personal character without consent of a person who has drawn up the written text without consent of a person shown on the portrait, photograph or film, or the voice of whom is recorded on a phonogram or without consent of another person the consent of whom is required by law, and thereby considerably violates the privacy of life of that person, shall be sentenced to a fine or imprisonment not exceeding one year. Article 176 provides for the protection of the unauthorized collection of personal data. It provides that a person who, in contradiction with law, collects personal data or utilizes so-collected data or anyone who provides, communicates to others or uses without permission personal data that are collected, processed, and utilized in line with law, for purposes other than those for which they were compiled, shall be sentenced to a fine or imprisonment not exceeding one year. Had any of these crimes (infringement of privacy of mail and other means of communications, unauthorized wiretapping and recording, unauthorized photographing, unauthorized publication, and presentation of a somebody else's written texts, portraits and recordings, and unauthorized collection of personal data) be committed by a person acting in an official capacity, during performance of his/her duties, that person shall be sentenced to imprisonment not exceeding three year. However, the last amendments on the Criminal Code, provides that the person, "who committed any of these crimes to prevent or detect crime sentenced with five years or more, will not be punished" (Article 176a). Therefore, when these acts are done as preventive investigation of any crime sentenced with five years or more, according to law, there is no technical authorization required for the person committing them.

118. Although defamation has been removed from the Criminal Code, the act of spreading information about private and family life of the activities of many international and national NGO's has remained a crime (Article 197). According to the Criminal Code, whoever spreads or transmits information about the personal or family life of a person and thereby potentially harms his/her honor or reputation shall be punished by a fine in the amount of EUR 3,000 to EUR 10,000. If the crime is committed through media or other similar means or at a public gathering, the perpetrator shall be punished by a fine in the amount of EUR 5,000 to EUR 14,000. Had this crime entailed or could have entailed serious consequences for the injured party, the perpetrator shall be punished by a fine in the minimum amount of EUR 8,000. However, this text prescribes that if the accused person has spread or transmitted information about personal or family life when performing an official duty, as a journalist engaged in his or her profession, or when defending a right or protecting a justified interest, s/he shall not be punished provided s/he proves that the information is true or that s/he had founded reasons to believe that the information s/he disclosed or transmitted is true.

119. Principle VII of the Codex of Montenegrin Journalists specifies that a journalist is obliged to be very careful when dealing with the private lives of people. A right to private life is disproportional to the importance of a public office that an individual holds, but in those cases too, it is necessary to respect human dignity. In the Guidelines for interpreting the principle VII, it is stipulated that a journalist should not intrude into and report on a person's private life without his or her consent and that the public's right to information must always be weighed against the personal rights of those involved. It further specifies that reporting on a person's private life can be justified when it is in the public interest to do so, i.e., detecting or exposing criminal conduct; detecting or exposing seriously anti-social conduct; protecting public health and safety; corruption, etc. Reporting on a person's private life is also justified if it prevents the public from being misled by some statement or action by that individual such as where a person is doing something in private which he or she is publicly condemning. In the case of public officials, journalists are entitled to probe his/her life when reporting deals with his or her suitability for the assignment he/she performs or aspires to perform. Regarding the victims of accidents or crimes, the guidelines provide special protection of their names. Exceptions can be justified if the person concerned is a public figure or if there are special accompanying circumstances. In the case of dependents and other people who are indirectly affected by an accident or who have nothing to do with a crime, care must be taken when publishing names and images. Publishing people's private addresses enjoy special protection. Also, physical and mental illness or injury fundamentally come within the private sphere of the persons affected. Out of consideration for them and their dependents, the media should not publish names and photographs in such cases and should avoid using disparaging terms to describe their illness, even if they are terms in popular usage. When reporting on suicides, special care has to be demonstrated, particularly, when media publish the names and detailed descriptions of the circumstances. Exceptions are justifiable only if the case is of public interest. If person is depicted only as the object, then the report shall be considered sensational, particularly if it reports on dying or physically or mentally suffering persons. The reports on accidents and disasters shall be considered acceptable as long as it reflects the respect for the suffering of the victims and the feelings of their dependents. Victims of misfortune must not be made to suffer a second time by their portrayal in the media.

120. None of the guaranteed rights can ever be absolutely enjoyed without limitations. On the contrary, as general postulate in law states that rights can be exercised up to the infringement of other internationally recognized rights. In fact, overconsumption of one's rights often means restriction of other right. The most pressing situations occur when two equally strong rights collide—the rights of media and the press and with internationally established legal right of individual's privacy. From the perspective of this clash that occurs within the context of these two guaranteed crucial freedoms, accordingly there are at least two crucial legal issues that are to be explained in light of the national legislative texts: " 1) freedom of expression as the pillar of any democratic society and the 2) right to privacy, defined under legal instruments as the limiting factor on the scope and definition of the freedom of expression."[97] However, one must not unreasonably restrict any conventional right. According to the regulations, declared and guaranteed human rights must not be restricted only to the extent necessary to comply with another right of the same power. Thus, every right, including freedom of expression is limited, but in the manner and under circumstances prescribed by law.[98]

121. The media often violate people's privacy by referring to unilateral interpretation of the right to freedom of expression as guaranteed by Article 10 of the European Convention on Human Rights. However, it is necessary to find a way to balance these two fundamental rights, both guaranteed by the European Convention on Human Rights: the right to respect for one's private life and the right to freedom of expression. Therefore, a proceeding that involves a minor has to absolutely adhere to the principle of confidentiality. This has been determined as the vital interest in

97. Spaic, A., Krone case, *supra.* , p. 11. Smet, S., *Freedom of Expression and the Right to Reputation: Human Rights in Conflict*, 26 Am. U. Int'l L. Rev. 1, 190 (2010).
98. Smet, S. *supra.*, p. 190.

ensuring fair trial without intimidation and victimization of the child. When seen and analyzed through the lenses of the most susceptible, social vulnerable group—minors—the conflict between these two rights must be more strictly scrutinized. For example, national laws, usually, make it unclear whether the media has restricted access to judicial proceedings. The legal issues surrounding media coverage of and access to, juvenile proceedings involve whether the media would be willing to accept certain conditions on their ability to publish information regarding minor. This potential collision has to be understood from the perspective of the freedom of the press, including media coverage, and the juvenile's right to privacy. The European Court of Human Rights, analyzing all national available legal instruments, decided in the *Krone Verlag GmbH v. Austria, ECtHR Judgement* (June 19, 2012) Application No. 27306/07 in favor of the juvenile's right to privacy, holding that the public policy reason was not present for the eventual disclosure of the identity of the juvenile.[99]

99. Spaic, A., Krone case, *supra.* , p. 11.

Chapter 4. Right to Reply

122. The right to reply has been strongly rooted in the Montenegrin legislative system. Constitution of Montenegro, Article 49 paragraph 2 states that "The right to a response and the right to a correction of any untrue, incomplete or incorrectly conveyed information that violates a person's right or interest and the right to compensation of damage caused by the publication of untruthful data or information shall be guaranteed." In addition to it, Criminal Code Article 180 stipulates the crime on prevention of publication of responses and rectifications. In fact, it states that anyone who, contrary to the final decision by a court of law, rejects or prevents to publicize a response or rectification of an incorrectly published information which violates someone's rights or interests, shall be sentenced to a fine or imprisonment not exceeding one year.

123. With respect to the electronic media, Article 47 of the Law on Electronic Media ("LEM") provides that the general rules in media law will apply regarding the procedure and the right to reply to information. The nature and conditions of invoking the right to reply are defined under the Articles 26–35 of the Media Law ("ML"). Under ML, a reply is an information which denies, essentially correct or supplement statements in the publicized program. In fact, it determines that each natural or legal person whose constitutional right(s) has/ve been violated in the publicized program is entitled a right to reply, free of charge.

124. Reply may be requested from the media who published program content but also from the founder of the medium or his legal successor of the medium which stopped working. In that case reply will be ensured by the medium of the similar features to the medium that stopped working, at the expense of the founder or legal successor of the medium which stopped working. There are two conditions that have to be fulfilled: (1) it has to be requested not later than thirty days from the day of publishing the programming; (2) it shall be stated which programming the reply refers to as well as the date of its publishing.

125. The reply shall be publicized in the first or the second print or broadcast media programming. The reply has to be published in the certain way: (1) Without any modification or addition and in the same column or a broadcast medium's program, which published the programming, related to reply; (2) In proportional length of the programming or a part of the programming it refers to.

126. As specified under Article 26, the medium is obliged to publish a reply to the published programming, unless one of the following situations occurred: "if a reply does not refer to the programming which was the reason for claiming their publishing or does not contain actual data referring to the claims published in the programming; if a reply denies the content of a published programming whose authenticity was verified by a valid decision of a competent authority; if a reply was submitted by a person the programming does not refer to; if a reply to the same programming has already been published at the request of the authorized person or if the reaction of the authorized person of the same content as the submitted correction or reply has already been published in the same medium, in some other equally valid form (interview, statement, etc.); if reply to the same program was submitted, with the same content as the earlier one, and the proceedings with regard to publishing of the earlier submitted correction or reply is not finished; if reply does not refer to the programming, which the person claims to be correcting or replying to; if the reply is such that its publishing would result in medium distribution banning, criminal or penal accountability, or civil legal accountability toward third persons; if reply was not signed by a person authorized by a legal person or if a natural person who submitted reply failed to write his identity card number and residential address on it; if reply disproportionately exceeds the length of a related programming and a submitter thereof rejects the written claim of editor in chief of the medium requesting appropriate shortening of the reply" (Article 26).

127. If the media outlet rejects to publish the reply, civil procedures can be initiated by the competent court against the founder of the medium, within thirty days from the deadline set for publishing reply. The media outlet is requested to submit all facts—materials relevant to the obligation of the medium to publish reply (copy or duplicate of printed issue, sound or video recording of the broadcast programming). Depending on the courts findings, media outlet will be ordered to publish the reply in due time and manner, when the complaint is accepted.

128. This court's judgment might be appealed not later than five days from the date of delivery. The Court of Appeals shall decide upon appeal, not later than five days from the date of receiving the appeal. The attested copy of the final judgment shall be submitted to the medium, which is obliged to keep all texts or broadcast recordings for at least thirty days upon their publication and to make them available to persons who have right to reply.

129. The right to reply is also determined in the Codex of Montenegrin Journalists in the following manner. Principle IV of the Codex of Montenegrin Journalists, 2016 specifies the duty of a journalist to correct/complete previous incomplete/incorrect information especially the one that can cause any harm and at the same time to make sure that the correction is pointed out in the adequate manner. In fact, in its Guidelines, it states that if a media outlet has published a report containing a significant distortion of the facts, it must publish a correction promptly in the same space or within the same program (with due/comparable prominence). Also, when media has published an erroneous report that has caused harm to a person's or institution's reputation, it must publish an apology promptly and with due prominence. In addition to it, it specifies that media outlet concerned must give the person or organization a fair opportunity to reply, to correct any inaccuracies and to respond to the criticism, when a person or organization believes that a media report contains inaccurate information or has unfairly criticized the person or organization. Media institution is expected to provide such right in the case of acceptance that the report in question had errors and unfounded allegations. Media outlet is obliged to change these issues in its archives, documentations, and data bases.

Chapter 5. Access to Public Information

130. One of the cornerstones of a democratic society is the right to information and the public's right to receive information of public interest. The current Law on Free Access to Information 2012, "approved" by the Venice Commission, precisely defines the concept and the procedure of obtaining the public information. The whole notion on the right to access information, however, has been rooted in the Constitution of Montenegro, 2007. Montenegro is member of the Council of Europe that signed the first international binding legal instrument—Convention on Access to Official Documents (CAOD) in 2009 and ratified it in 2012. The current law has been written in accordance with this Convention and European standards, especially regarding the procedure, introduction of the harm test, and monitoring and complaint procedure.

131. In fact all laws provide that the access to information is of public interest, and it may be restricted only in purpose of protecting the higher interests and aims. Access to information held by public authorities shall be based on the principles of free access to information, transparency in work of public authorities, the right of the public to know and equality of requests, and it shall be carried out at the level of standards set out in ratified international agreements on human rights and freedoms and in generally recognized rules of international law. Any entity shall be entitled to access the information, without stating the reasons for seeking for it. The public shall be given information which is of importance to forming opinions on the state of society and functioning of authorities, as well as for exercise of democratic control over authorities, and exercise of human rights and freedoms.

132. The procedure for access to information is defined within the Part III, Articles 18–45 of LFAI. Generally speaking, an applicant shall have the right to choose one of three forms of access to requested information by: (1) direct inspection of original or copy of information in premises of the public authority; (2) the applicant transcribing or scanning the information in the premises of a public authority; (3) delivery of a copy of the information to the applicant by hand, mail, or e-mail. Public authority shall grant the access to information in such a form, unless it is technically unfeasible (Article 24). The public authority that holds requested information shall be competent for deciding upon the request on access to information. However, if that information is published in Montenegro and available on the internet, it shall not be obliged to grant access to information. The applicant asking for the access to information can request it via written or verbal requests. The written request for access to information shall be submitted directly to the responsible authority by hand, mail, or e-mail (via fax, e-mail, etc.), whereas oral request might be sent via minutes/record. The Law, in Article 18, specifies that request for access shall contain the following information: the name of the information or data that allow its identification; the form in which the applicant wishes to access information; information on the applicant. During this process the public authority shall pay attention to the protection of such personal data that affect privacy and data that have been classified.

133. Right on access to information can be in the form of a document in written, print, video, audio, electronic, or any other form, including its copy or part thereof, regardless to content, source, date and time of composing or classification system. The right on access to information shall encompass the right to ask for and receive information, (regardless of purpose and data consisted thereof) held by public authorities (public information) in the Montenegrin national legal system is defined in the *lex specialis* Law on Free Access to Information.[100] In fact, state, local self-government authority, local administration authority, institution, company and any other legal person founded or co-founded by the state or in majority ownership of the state or local self-government, legal person mainly financed from public resources, as well as a natural person, entrepreneur, or legal person having public responsibilities or managing public funds are obliged to respond to the request of the person to have access to the public information. In fact, access to public information is of public interest and it shall be exercised in accordance with the principles of free access to information, transparency in work of public authorities, the right of the public to know and equality of requests, and it shall be carried out at the level of standards set out in ratified international agreements on human rights and freedoms and in generally recognized rules of international law.

134. Under Article 11, the public authority shall publish, and regularly update a (once a year) Guide for access to information held by it. It shall contain a catalog of all types of documents, including public registers and public records, the address and e-mail address for submission of request, contact telephone, information on responsible persons, information on costs of access to information, and other data that are of importance to the exercise of the right of access to information held by the public authority. It further states that the public authority shall publish on its website following information: "the access to information guide; public registries and public records; programmers and work plans; reports and other documents on work and state of play in areas within their competence; drafts, proposals, and final texts of strategic documents, plans, and programmers for their implementation; draft and proposal of laws and other regulations, as well as opinions of experts delivered in relation to drafts and proposals for legislation; single acts and contracts on use of financial resources originating from public revenues and of state-owned property; list of civil servants and state employees with their titles; list of public officials and pay lists for them, as well as list of other incomes related to exercise of public function; decisions and other single acts that are of importance to rights, duties, and interests of third parties; information to which the access was granted upon request for more than three times" (Article 12).

135. Although, all highest legal acts such as the Constitution, obligatory international treaties and bylaws, establish the right to access information, none of the guaranteed rights can ever be enjoyed absolutely, meaning without limitations. On the contrary, as a general postulate in law, the right can be exercised up to the infringement of other recognized rights. The Constitution under Article 51 provides that everyone shall have the right to access information held by the state authorities and organizations exercising public authority, but it may be limited if this is in the interest of: the protection of life; public health; morality and privacy; carrying of criminal proceedings; security and defense of Montenegro; foreign, monetary, and economic policy. However, one must not unreasonably restrict freedom of expression, either through misuse by the public or by private authority.

100. Law on Free Access to Information (OG of MNE, No. 44/12).

136. The amendment of the Law of 2012, has introduced the harm test which determines whether the requested information can be disclosed to public. The general rules state that the access to information shall be restricted if disclosure of information would significantly jeopardize certain interests, or if there is a possibility that disclosure of information would cause harm to interest that is greater than the interest of the public to know that information, unless there is prevailing public interest.

137. The Law provides on the specific grounds under which the public authority might restrict the access to information. These grounds are: "1) protection of privacy from disclosure of personal data envisaged in the law regulating protection of data on individual, except for data relating to following: persons exercising public function, data relating to the public function exercise, as well as to incomes, property and conflict of interest of those persons and their relatives covered by the law regulating preventing of conflict of interest; resources allocated from the public funds, except those for social security benefits, health care, and protection against unemployment; 2) security, defense, foreign, monetary and economic policy of Montenegro, in accordance with the laws regulating the field of data secrecy, classified with certain level of confidentiality; 3) prevention of investigation and criminal prosecution, in order to protect from disclosure data referring to following: to prevent committing the criminal act, on reporting criminal act and perpetrator of it, on content of actions undertaken in pre-trial and criminal procedure; data collected through observation and investigation, on secret surveillance measures; on protected witness and collaborators of justice; efficient conducting of procedure; 4) performing the official duty, in order to protect from disclosure data referring to following: planning of inspection control and supervision by the public authority, consultations within and between public authorities regarding defining the positions and development of official documents and proposals for resolution of a case, work and decision making by collegial bodies; bringing and conduct of disciplinary proceedings; and 5) protection of private and commercial interest from disclosure of data relating to protection of competition and business secret in relation to intellectual property right" (Article 14).

138. Article 15 provides that restriction of access to information for the purpose of protecting privacy and data on protected witness and collaborator of justice shall last seventy years from the day of production, and at least twenty years following the demise of a person to whom the information relates, except in case that concerned person, or his/her spouse, children, or parents' consent to earlier publication of information. Restrictions of access to information for the purpose of protection of security, defense, foreign, monetary, and economic policies of Montenegro may last not later than until the expiry of the timeframes set by the law governing data secrecy. Restrictions of access to information for the prevention of investigation and criminal prosecution shall last by the latest until the procedure is completed. Restrictions of access to information for the purpose of performing official duty shall last until the official document is prepared, or proposed solution for the case is defined, minutes of the meeting of collegial body is verified, and disciplinary procedure is completed. Restrictions of access to information for the purpose of protecting private and commercial interests shall last until the expiry of the timeframes set by the law governing intellectual property rights.

139. The public authority shall decide upon a request for access to information containing classified data after obtaining a previous consent of the authority that proclaimed information as classified. Within eight working days as of receiving a request for consent, the classifying authority shall decide upon the request for information access. The law provides that prevailing public interest for disclosure of information exists when the requested information contains data on: corruption, non-observance of regulations, unauthorized use of public funds, or abuse of authority in exercising public function; the existence of grounds to believe that a criminal offense has been committed or existence of reasons to challenge a court decision; illegal receiving or spending of funds originating from public revenues; threats to public security; threats to life; threats to public health; threats to the environment. The public authority shall grant the access to information or part of information in cases when there is prevailing public interest for disclosure of information, unless it proves the existence of other prevailing public interest. The harm test shall not be applied to data contained in information that is proclaimed as classified by the foreign state or an international organization; such information remains inaccessible. These two exceptions, according to the Venice commission Opinion, are in the line with the European standards.

140. As provided in the Articles 34–38 and 44, the law ensures the process and appeals against decisions of public authorities by an independent supervisory body—Agency for the Protection of Personal Data and Access to Information (APPDAI). This Agency has the jurisdiction in deciding in submitting the requests for opening of misdemeanor proceedings for violations of LFAI that relates to: developing and updating the Access to information Guide, proactive publishing of information, and delivery of acts and data necessary for keeping an information system for access to information (Article 39(5)). In fact, it is specified that the Council of the Agency which shall make a decision *in meritum* upon the complaint against a decision on the request for access to information. The legal grounds for submitting the complaint are: (a) incomplete and incorrect factual statements; and (b) violations of material and procedural law. The confidential information cannot be decided by the Agency, due to the Agency's incapacity to assess whether information is properly marked as secret. Court protection is ensured against all final decisions on access to information. The court has the exclusive jurisdiction regarding the information containing data marked as confidential.[101]

141. Under Article 48 of the Law on Free Access to Information, if the Agency on the Protection fails to: (1) make a decision about a complaint and submit it to the applicant within fifteen days of the day on which the complaint is submitted or fails to decide *in meritum* on complaint against a decision on access to information (Venice Commission noted that the period of fifteen days is unrealistically short); (2) submit a report to the Parliament on the state of play in the area of access to information, the Agency will be fined (from EUR 200 to EUR 2,000). The same fine (from EUR 500 to EUR 20,000) shall be imposed upon the public authority violating the Law on Free Access to information.

---

101. European Commission For Democracy Through Law (Venice Commission), Draft Law On Free Access To Information Of Montenegro, Version Of April 2012.

142. This law was approved by the Venice Commission which found that vast majority of the provisions are in full compliance with the CAOD.[102]

§1. Public Documents and Meetings

143. In accordance with the constitutionally proclaimed right to access information held by public bodies and organizations exercising public authority Montenegro, the right to report on court hearing and documents has been strongly incorporated into Montenegrin law (Article 51 paragraph 1 of the Constitution of Montenegro). On the other hand the Constitution in Article 43 guarantees the protection of personal data, and thereby limits the access to information (Article 51 paragraph 2). The potential collisions, as well as the ratio between these two rights are regulated in details by the Law on free access to information.

144. As provided in Articles 3 of LFAI, any national or foreign entity is entitled to access to public document has the right to seek the information. Access to public information shall ensure the transparency, efficiency, effectiveness, and accountability, right of public to be informed and to know information held by the public authority. All these aspects are relevant in forming of opinions on state, society, authorities, and society in general.

145. Rulebooks on Programme Standards in Electronic Media (RPSEM), in Articles 7–11, provide that broadcasters that produce news programs are obliged to inform the public in a professional and responsible manner and to convey information to the public about the events in the country and abroad in a free, accurate, comprehensive, impartial, and timely manner. Article 8 of RPSEM states the obligation of the electronic media, in producing of news programmers, to observe the principles of objectivity, impartiality, timeliness, accuracy, non-discrimination, freedom to comment, and hear the other side rule. The events shall be presented accurately, and different approaches and opinions shall be represented in a professional and fair manner. Opinions and comments shall be separated from the factual reporting, and their source or author shall be clearly recognizable. At a written request of the public administration authorities or a public institution, the broadcasters are obliged to publish, free of charge, the announcements and official press releases, in case of danger for the lives and health of people, national security, or public order.

146. In addition, Montenegrin law specifies that radio or television broadcasts shall meet the following requirements: events shall be realistically shown; news shall truly and accurately present facts and events, shall be impartial and professionally accurate; opinions and comments shall be separated and their source or author recognizable; impartiality shall be encouraged, respecting the difference of opinion on political or economic matters. Under Article 55(1), a broadcaster is free, true, integral, impartial, and timely information of the public of events in the country and abroad.

147. Within the general principles of the Codex of Montenegrin Journalists of 2016, under its Guidelines, there is the rule on the Rallies during Election Campaign.

102. European Commission For Democracy Through Law (Venice Commission), Draft Law On Free Access To Information Of Montenegro, Version Of April 2012.

When reporting from rallies organized during an election campaign, the reporters will also report on the views and values with which they may not agree. Such an approach is a matter of reporter's fairness; it serves the citizens' right to the freedom of information and supports the principle of equal opportunities for all political parties and other participants in the election process.

§2. Court Hearings and Documents

148. Media outlets and journalists are obliged to report on the court proceedings in a specific - objective and true manner, as provided in the several legislative pieces: Media Law, Law on Liability of Legal Entities for Criminal Offenses, Criminal Code, Law on Contracts and Torts, Law on Free Access to Information, Journalists' Code of Ethics of 2016 and Rulebook on the Programme Standards in Electronic Media, the Supreme Court Opinion on the meaning and the scope of the free access to the court decisions.[103]

149. Media Law defines that if a media outlet informs that criminal charges have been brought against a certain person, that person might request (not later than thirty days) the publication of the information on the dismissal of charges or the end of criminal proceedings. The media is not obliged to publish the information if the request for publicizing the information was not accompanied by a final decision on the suspension of criminal proceedings. Law on Liability of Legal Entities for Criminal Offenses states that "Court shall impose the safety measure of publishing the judgment if it believes it would be useful to inform the public about the judgment, particularly if the judgment publication would contribute to eliminate a threat to life or health of people or to protect the safety of trade or other general interest" (Article 31).[104] It further determines that the court has the authority to select the media that will publish the judgment. In fact, depending on the relevance of the criminal offense, need to inform the public, and interest of whom the judgment should be published, the Court also decides on whether the decision would be published completely or in the form of an extract.

150. In the same manner, the Criminal Code of Montenegro, in Article 77, specifies that "when pronouncing a sentence for criminal offences committed by means of public media, the court can decide to publish the judgment either fully or in brief through the media and at the offender's expense. Mandatory publishing of the judgment can be prescribed by law." In that case, the court shall decide which media outlet will

103. Media Law (OG of MNE, Nos. 82/08, 51/02, 362/02), Law on Liability of Legal Entities For Criminal Offenses (OG of MNE, No. 70/03, 13/04), Criminal Code (OG of MNE, No. 70/03, 13/04, 47/06, 40/08, 25/10, 32/11, 40/13, 56/13, 014/14, 042/15, 058/15), Law on Free Access to Information (OG of MNE, No. 44/12), Rulebooks on Programme Standards in Electronic Media (OG of MNE, Nos. 46/10, 007/16), Supreme Court Opinion on the meaning and the scope of the free access to the court decisions, Bulletin 2011, The Supreme Court of Montenegro, ISNN 1800-5810.

104. Nolasco, C., Spaic, A., Vaughn, M.S., *Media Access to Juvenile Proceedings: Balancing the Tightrope Between Privacy Rights and Freedom of the Press*, 43 Int'l J.L., Crime & Just. 4, 643–675.

publish the part or the whole judgment, within thirty days of the day the judgment became effective. Montenegrin Criminal Code provides for the crime on prevention of publication of responses and rectifications (Article 180). It states that anyone who, contrary to the final decision by a court of law, rejects or prevents to publicize a response or rectification of an incorrectly published information which violates someone's rights or interests, shall be sentenced to a fine or imprisonment not exceeding one year. In the same Code, in Article 391, the Montenegrin legislator has stipulated several legal situations in which the violation of confidentiality of procedure has been breached. For example, it states that whoever discloses without authorization information obtained in court shall be punished by either a fine or imprisonment for a maximum term of one year. It prescribes that this punishment shall also be imposed on a person who, without the permission of the court, publicizes the course of the criminal procedure taken against juveniles, or the name of a juvenile or the data revealing identity of the juvenile. Also, if someone without authorization discloses information on the identity or personal data of persons protected in criminal proceedings or special protection program, they shall be punished with imprisonment up to three years. If this conduct results in serious consequences for the protected person or the criminal proceedings had been suspended or significantly aggravated, the offender shall be punished with imprisonment from six months to five years.

151. Also, the Law on Contracts and Torts does not stay silent either. Article 206 of the Law on Contracts and Torts states that in case of violation of an individual right, the court may order that, at the expense of the tortfeasor, the sentence, namely the correction, be made public, or it may order that the tortfeasor take back the statement causing the violation, or order something else which would reach the purpose, otherwise apt to be achieved by indemnity.

152. In applying the Law on Free Access to Information on court decisions, courts act differently. The constitutional right to access information, the principle of transparency of the courts and obligation to publish decisions on the website, are the main features of the standardized practice of all Montenegrin courts. However, the Supreme Court brought an Opinion on the meaning and the scope of the free access to the courts' decisions. Access to court records cannot be made on the basis of the Law on Free Access to Information, but solely on the basis of procedural laws (Criminal Procedure Code, the Law on Civil Procedure, Law on Administrative Conflict) and the Law on Courts. When the access to non-published court decisions is sought, under the Law on Free Access to Information, the competent court is obliged to provide access to information by submitting the required decisions after they complete anonymization of data in accordance with the Rules on anonymization of data in judicial decisions. If the requested final and enforceable decisions are already published on the website of the competent court, the court shall refuse a request for access to information at the same time inform the applicant of the carrier of the required information. The Supreme Court Opinion also states that request of the individual, exact or certain court decision which can exposed the personal data info, will be rejected.[105]

105. Opinion of Supreme Court on the meaning and the scope of the free access to the courts decisions, Bulletin 2011, The Supreme Court of Montenegro, ISNN 1800-5810.

153. Principle IX of the Journalists' Code of Ethics of 2016 states that when reporting on investigation and court procedures, a journalist has to respect the assumption that everyone is innocent until proven otherwise and should by no means pre-adjudicate the outcome of a court procedure. Regarding this principle IX the Guidelines of the Codex emphasize three pillars: (1) Reporting on Criminals, investigations, and court procedures; (2) Reporting acts of violence; and (3) Coordination with the authorities/ news "blackouts." With respect to the first one, Guideline provides detailed regulation stating that: "(a) Reports on investigations and court cases serve to inform the public about prosecution and court judgment, stating that a person is presumed innocent until proven guilty by a court, even if he or she has confessed or the guilt is obvious to the public; (b) Prejudicial portrayals and allegations violate the constitutional protection of human dignity, which also applies without qualification to criminals. The aim of court reporting must not be to punish convicted criminals socially publicly via media; (c) Where a media has started reporting a criminal case, it must also report subsequent developments. If the media reported the name or other identifiable data, it should also report an acquittal or lessening of charges or dropping of an investigation; (d) Criticism and comment on a case must be easily distinguishable from reporting on court proceedings; (e) Unless the victims have consented or media was authorized, media must not directly or indirectly identify victims of sexual assaults; (f) The media should generally avoid identifying relatives or friends convicted or accused of crime unless the reference to them is necessary for the full, fair, and accurate reporting of the crime or the legal proceedings; (g) When reporting on investigations and criminal proceedings against minors, the media must exercise a special restraint out of consideration for their future."

154. Under Articles 28–31 of Rulebooks on Programme Standards in Electronic Media (RPSEM), court, secrecy of proceeding, as well as presumption of innocence have been adopted as the special program standard in the electronic media programmers. Media outlets are obliged to cover the judicial proceedings in an objective and accurate manner, providing the information on court decisions, especially if the charges are dismissed, an investigation is suspended, or the gravity of offense the defendant is charged with is reduced. During the criminal proceedings, the electronic media are obliged to observe the right to privacy of all persons involved in the proceedings in any capacity. Identity of the victims of sexual assault shall not be revealed either directly or by publishing the material that could result in the revealing of their identity, unless the victims give their consent or in case there is prior approval of the competent authority. Electronic media are obliged to have particular regard to the protection of minors and other vulnerable persons, as well as victims, witnesses, and families of the suspects, defendants, or convicted persons. The electronic media are obliged to have regard to the protection of identity of witnesses. Identity of witnesses may be revealed only in the cases when: a witness gives prior consent; the revealing of identity serves public interest; the testimony was public. The RPSEM further state that electronic media are obliged to pay particular attention to the observance of the rights and obligations of the protected or endangered witnesses, as well as the members of their families. It is prohibited to publish any information that could have obvious negative effect on the course of judicial proceedings, and the information the secrecy of which has been explicitly requested by the court before or during the proceedings. Live coverage from a courtroom or recording in a courtroom is allowed only with prior authorization of the competent judicial authorities.

155. In March 2016, the Special State Prosecutor requested the amendments of the Law on the Special Prosecutor Office. This amendment has extended the already existing crime of "violation of the secrecy of the proceedings." Publishing the information and data from the reconnaissance and investigation procedure, without the prior approval from the Special State Prosecutor, will constitute a violation of the secrecy of the proceedings. Although, the purpose of this provision is legitimate, it has been written in a pretty strong tone advocating for the situation in which media outlets are prevented to report. In the majority of liberal democracies, this provision is drafted in a manner so that media presumably has the right to report on these procedures, unless a gag order has been issued. At the moment, this amendment is waiting for its adoption in the Parliament of Montenegro.

Chapter 6. Press Council

156. The concept of media self-regulation is the crucial concept for ensuring ethical and professional standards, editorial freedom, and credibility of journalists in all democratic countries all over the world. In majority of these countries, media self-regulation for media outlets has been ensured through proper functioning of this body. In countries with a strong self-regulatory bodies, the practice of false reporting, spinning, unfair and untimely informing are relentlessly condemned. The idea of setting up a unique institution with the purpose of providing unbiased analysis of variety of media outlet contents, has not yet been realized in Montenegro.[106] After the first adoption of its Journalists Code, for the first time, after several years, the National Journalist Body in Montenegro, was established in 2003. Montenegrin journalists have struggled to establish a common self-regulatory body since then. The self-regulatory body established in 2003 ceased to exist in 2010 as a sole institution. The lack of a sole national self-regulatory institution contributes to the chaotic atmosphere in the media arena.

157. Montenegrin media community was divided over the creation of one unique institution responsible for monitoring professional and ethical standards in journalism.[107] At present, several active self-regulatory bodies exist in Montenegro. These are: Media self-regulatory body (MSB), self-regulatory Council for local and periodical newspapers in Montenegro, Ombudsman with TV Vijesti and Ombudsman with Dan. The biggest among them—MSB, covering 90% of the media outlets functioning in Montenegro, has the role of conducting mediation between defamed and injured individuals and media outlets. It consists of three bodies: Executive Secretary, Managing Board, and the Commission for Monitoring and Complaints.

158. The new MSB was registered in March 2012. It has nineteen print, broadcast and Internet media outlets participating (TV CRNE GORE, RTV ATLAS, POBJEDA, DNEVNE NOVINE, TV MBC, Radio ELMAG, TV TEUTA, TV BOIN, Radio ANTENA M, Radio SKALA, Radio TIVAT, Radio DUX, Portal ANALITIKA, Portal CAFFE DEL MONTENEGRO, Radio JADRAN, Radio CRNE GORE, Portal RTM, TV Prva, TV Pink M). It does not, however, include three relevant media outlets such as "Dan," "Vijesti," and the weekly "Monitor."[108]

159. In April 2016, under the auspices of the Council of Europe and the Office of the OSCE, Montenegro adopted the Journalists' Code of Ethics of 2016. Its adoption has been deemed a significant step toward improving the media's overall environment

106. Network for Affirmation of NGO Sector (MANS), "How much does it cost for a journalist to be critical in Montenegro?", p. 5, available at: http://www.mans.co.me/en/wp-content/uploads/fai/FreedomOfExpression-Internship.pdf).
107. Montenegro Progress Report, Enlargement Strategy and Main Challenges 2014–2015, COM (2014) 700 final, p. 44, Network for Affirmation of NGO Sector (MANS), "How much does it cost for a journalist to be critical in Montenegro?", p. 5, available at: http://www.mans.co.me/en/wp-content/uploads/fai/FreedomOfExpression-Internship.pdf, CEDEM and OSCE, Socijalni položaj novinarske profesije u Crnoj Gori, November 2014, available at: http://sindikatmedija.me/images/pdf/osceizvjestaj.pdf.
108. Freedom of House Annaul Report, 2014, available at: https://freedomhouse.org/report/freedom-press/2014/montenegro#.VcwUuWCFPIU.

and self-regulation in Montenegro. The OSCE Mission in Montenegro has strongly insisted on the adoption of the Codex. Codex shall "pave the way to polarized media outlets to get together and start working on keeping up the professional standards in reporting." Although, Montenegro has adopted Code of Journalists of Montenegro, freedom of expression through the functioning of media self-regulation in Montenegro has not yet strongly contributed to raising awareness and protection of the public interest.[109] The enhancement of the media environment can be accomplished only by strong commitment of all actors: academic society, lawyers, journalists, but also of the lay public.

109. Zečević M., Tasić S., *Medijski savjet za samoregulaciju se bori da se pozicionira kao kredibilan i snažan mehanizam samoregulacije medijskog sadržaja*, available at http://www.fairpress.eu/me/blog/2014/11/17/medijski-savjet-za-samoregulaciju-se-bori-da-se-pozicionira-kao-kredibilan-i-snazan-mehanizam-samoregulacije-medijskog-sadrzaja/, Monitoring novinarskih samoregulatornih tijela u Crnoj Gori, Prvi izvještaj (2012–2013) available at http://www.hraction.org/wp-content/uploads/FIN-Monitoring-zakljucki-i-preporuke.pdf, pp. 1–4.

Part III. Regulation of Audiovisual Media (Broadcasting)

160. The rights, duties, and responsibilities of different categories of legal and natural persons pursuing the activities of audiovisual media (hereafter: AVM), as well as the conditions for their registrations are defined under the Law on Electronic Media Law.[110] In fact, it stipulates that after obtaining a broadcasting license, a legal or a natural person with the status of a broadcaster may produce and transmit radio and/or television programs. A broadcaster may generate it in the form of: a public broadcaster, a commercial broadcaster; and a non-for-profit broadcaster.

161. Article 7 of LEM, specifies the obligation of the Government of Montenegro to adopt the Development Programme for AVM service sector. The Council of the AEM shall approve the draft Development Programme for AVM services sector, and shall submit it to the government for adoption. The Programme shall contain in particular: vision; goals, and objectives; means of attaining goals and objectives; timeframe, expected development of structures and types of AVM service providers, as well as other issues relevant for the development of the AVM services sector.

110. Law on Electronic Media (OG of MNE, Nos. 46/10, 40/11, 53/11, 055/16).

Chapter 1. Public Service Broadcasting

§1. The Concept and Mission of PSB

162. After the collapse of communism in Yugoslavia, the influence of the Western media culture as well as the rise of capitalism has generated the changes in media environment in Montenegro. Media pluralism has emerged at first in the form of dividing the media outlets between the government and its opposition. Only in the 1990s has Montenegro witnessed the generation of the first independent print media outlet. At the same time, Montenegro, as well as other post-communist countries, has faced the dilemma whether to keep state media or to transform it into a new public media sector. Under the auspices of the EU, Montenegro responded by transforming it into the PSB. It has applied the known model of budget financing (state intervention model). Media theorists and practitioners have condemned this form of public financing, alleging that this hinders some of the significant features of a PSB, namely: independency from the government and the impartiality of the program.[111]

163. PSB of Montenegro consists of RTM. Their production is aimed at addressing social, educational, cultural, and other needs of public interest of all segments of Montenegrin society, regardless of political, religious, cultural, race, or sex affiliations of all Montenegrin citizens. These activities are conducted by means of a terrestrial network of FM and AM transmitters at the national level, two television programs of the Television of Montenegro by means of a terrestrial transmission network at the national level, broadcasting its radio and television programs by means of satellite, and transmitting and broadcasting the RTM program Parliamentary Television by means of radio frequencies and electronic communications networks. Every territory of Montenegro populated by at least 85% of the citizens must be provided the reception of RTM programs, within every radio or television network. Article 4 of the LPSB, states that RTM may broadcast RTM programs also via internet. If it is of interest to citizens, RTM may produce and broadcast other radio and television programs, in compliance with the law. Neither a change of the main activity nor the privatization of RTM can be done without the consent of the Parliament of Montenegro.

164. LPSB, in Article 9, specifies that RTM has several legally prescribed duties to: serve in strengthening community and integrating of all individuals, groups and communities; meet local and national public interests and needs in broadcasting informative, cultural, educational, scientific, sport and entertaining programs; affirm and foster Montenegrin identity by broadcasting national and cultural identity, cultural and ethnic identity of national and ethnic minorities, European cultural heritage and cultural diversity; promote free expression of different opinions and positions on issues of public interest; generate program of the child well-being, national and ethnic minorities, disabled persons, socially vulnerable groups, and other specific groups; affirm Montenegrin cultural heritage, foster and encourage cultural and art work, and widen knowledge on different cultures presented in Montenegro; reflect different ideas

111. Barendt, E., *Freedom of Speech*. 2nd ed., p. 13 Oxford University Press, New York, 2005.

and religious beliefs in society, aimed at strengthening of understanding, tolerance and promoting of multicultural, multiethnic and multi-confessional society of Montenegro; promote fundamental human rights and freedoms, democratic values and institutions, and pluralism of ideas, public dialogue culture, linguistic standards, privacy and dignity of individuals; promote and urge democratic culture of society; promote civil society values, strengthen citizens' initiative; generate the program of the on the events and matters of public importance; reflect actual life problems of different structures in Montenegrin society; promote historical materials, produce the program on health, property, cultural heritage and environment; promote cinematographic and audiovisual works; promote development of ecologic state of Montenegro; provide equal presentation of political parties during the election campaign.

§2. The Organization of PSB

165. Along with the Law on Electronic Media (LEM), as the *lex generalis,* Law on PSB of Montenegro (LPSBM) is *lex specialis* for the regulation of public service. As already stated, PSB in Montenegro has two business and organizational units: "Radio of Montenegro" and "Television of Montenegro." RTM is liable to the public. Article 12 of LPSB states that the liability of RTM is ensured through: its adherence to professional standards and program rules; the procedure of appointment of the RTM Council; public work and duty to represent and protect citizens' interests in the field of information; informing the public about the RTM activities by means of publicizing the Operation Bulletin in print or/and electronic form; and, prescribing and implementing the procedures that enable the listeners and viewers to submit the petitions and complaints concerning the RTM work.

166. The founder of "RTM" is the State, whose rights and interests are protected by the Council of RTM. In fact, the state is the owner of all RTM assets. It consists of the ownership rights over movable assets and real estate, financial resources, securities, and other property rights. RTM is liable for its commitments with all of its assets, while the State has joint, several, and unlimited liability for the commitments of RTM. Furthermore, without the consent of the RTM Council, RTM cannot dispose of its assets.

167. Although the State is strongly involved in establishing of the RTM, it is expected to independently decide upon the content of the program, and in accordance with it shall: determine program scheme and concept of program, edit and broadcast information on current events and organize performing of the activities. RTM journalists shall be independent in their work and they shall act in the public interest. Under the Law, Statute and Code of Ethics, when acting in accordance with professional standards and program-related rules journalists have to be protected. In fact, when expressing their professional opinion they shall not suffer in any of the following ways: dismissal from a job, reduction of salary, removal from editorial post. RTM regulates its internal organization and manner of work through its two bodies: RTM Council and RTM Director General (Article 20 of the LPSB).

I. RTM Director General

168. Article 49 of the LPSB specifies the requirements for the RTM Director General. It determines that it shall be a person with Montenegrin citizenship, with a university degree minimum, the residence in Montenegro, and at least five years of professional experience. He is responsible for: acting for and representing RTM; organizing work; proposing different legal acts on determining program and professional standards and of the RTM; submitting report on work and periodical and annual statements of account of RTM, financial statement of RTM for previous year; signing the contract with the Ministry, ensuring realization of program-related documents and professional standards in the RTM; appointing and recalling Director of Radio of Montenegro and Director of Television of Montenegro, as well as other management staff in the RTM.

169. RTM Director General shall appoint/recall the Director of Radio of Montenegro and Director of Television of Montenegro. The same requirement relevant for the appointment of the Director General shall apply to all directors of Radio and Television on the same term of four years. Director of Radio of Montenegro, or Director of Television of Montenegro shall *inter alia*: act for and represent Radio of Montenegro or Television of Montenegro; propose the program orientation of Radio of Montenegro or Television of Montenegro, be accountable for the implementation of program to the RTM Council, enforce adopted operating plans of Radio of Montenegro or Television of Montenegro, etc.

170. All RTM directors, Director General, Director of Radio of Montenegro, and Director of Television of Montenegro may be recalled before the expiry of their term in the following situations: upon a personal request; if they fail to act in compliance with the provisions of law and general acts of RTM; if their negligent and irregular conduct leads to significant damage to RTM.

II. Advisory Body of RTM

171. As a body independent of any state authority, organizations, and persons involved in the activity of production and broadcasting of radio and television programs, advertising or telecommunications, the Council body of RTM shall only represent the common interests of the public (Articles 21–48 LPSB). The Council of RTM is an independent body with broad jurisdiction over 22 legal and factual competences in the area of adoption, appointment, approvals, and analysis relevant for the functioning of RTM. Its main activities, Article 22 of LPSB list them in the following manner: Adoption of the RTM Statute and general acts on program professional standards in RTM, internal organization and systematization of job positions, working plans, periodical, and annual statements of RTM account, deciding on the investment and financial plans of RTM, deciding on the purchase, sale and mortgaging of RTM property, appointment of the chairman, deputy chairman and RTM Director, auditor of periodic and annual statements of account of RTM, Commission for Petitions and Complaints, Commission of Programming in Albanian and Languages of Other National and Ethnic Groups, approval for contract on use of funds from Budget, Analysis and deciding upon violation of the program principles and proposal of appropriate measures to the Director of Radio of Montenegro or Director of Television of Montenegro.

172. RTM Council Member shall act independently, autonomously, according to their own knowledge and conscience, and in the public interest, and conform the law. Nobody has the right to influence, in any way, the work of the RTM Council Members, and they are not obliged to observe anybody's instructions with regard to their work, except the decisions of a competent Court. In order to contribute in ensuring its independent work, the Law stipulates relatively high compensation for their work, in Montenegrin terms. In fact, Members are entitled to a monthly compensation in amount of the one received by other employees in the RTM in the month prior to payment of compensation and reimbursement of the costs arising from performing of duties as the Council member (Article 31). As the body serving to the public interest, Article 23 specifies that the Council shall publish three reports every year, via the RTM website. First, report on the work of the RTM of the previous year, with special emphasis on the implementation of program standards and realization of obligations; second, report on financial operations of the RTM of the previous year; and third, report of the authorized auditor on financial operations of the RTM.

173. The RTM Council shall comprise of nine members, holders of a university level degree and esteemed expert in the field relevant for performing of activities of the RTM (media, law, economy, technical sciences, sociology, marketing, broadcasting, etc.). With regard of initiating the procedure for the RTM Council appointment, the law is precise. In fact, the whole process starts by issuing a public invitation for the authorized nominators which invites submission of proposals within forty-five days. The Parliament shall decide upon proposed list for the RTM Council appointment not later than within sixty days from the date of delivering material. If the proposed list is not complete, procedure shall be reopened from the category of nominator whose proposal is not adopted. The term of office of the RTM Council is five years, with the possibility of reelection one more time, while the termination might occur: upon the expiry of the term; by recall; by submission of written resignation to the Parliament, and upon the death of the member. RTM Council's work is regulated by the RTM Council Rules of Procedure Work. RTM Council sessions shall be held at least once a month and are usually open to the public. RTM Council Decisions shall be reached by majority vote of the RTM Council Members present (Article 48). Director General and Directors of Radio of Montenegro and Television of Montenegro, shall have the right to take part in the RTM Council sessions, without decision-making powers. However, a two-third members' vote can decide to exclude them.

174. Authorized nominators of the RTM Council Members such as Universities in Montenegro, Montenegrin Academy of Science and Art, and "Matica crnogorska," National institutions of culture and non-governmental organizations in field of culture, Montenegrin Chamber of Commerce and association of employers represented in the Social Council, non-governmental organizations in field of media, except for association of broadcasters, trade union represented in the Social Council, Montenegrin Olympic Committee and Montenegrin Para-Olympic Committee, have right to nominate one member, whereas non-governmental organizations for protection of human rights and freedoms, which deal with exercise and protection of national, gender and total equality; right on healthy environment; consumers' rights; rights of the disabled persons or right on education and social welfare have right to nominate two members. Proposal for appointment of the RTM Council member shall contain name and surname, address, short biography of the proposed candidate. Proposal shall be signed and submitted to the Parliament Working body along with the: Certificate on permanent residence in Montenegro of the nominated candidate and his/ hers completed education; Statement of the proposed candidate on acceptance of nomination, and on nonexistence of obstacles determined by law. Non-governmental organization, in position of the nominator, shall submit, together with certificates/evidences additional documents such as: Certificate on registration (registered for three years); Founding act and statute; Reports on work and financial reports for previous three years (Article 29 of the LPSB).

175. The list of the grounds for conflict of interest rule is broadly conceptualized so that a Member of the Council cannot be: member of the national Parliament and of the local assemblies; person elected, nominated, or appointed by the President of Montenegro, the Parliament of Montenegro, or the Government of Montenegro; RTM employees; officials of the political parties (president of the party, member of the presidency of the party, their deputies, members of executive and general committees of the party, and other party's officials); persons, who as stake holders, shareholders, members of managing bodies, members of supervisory bodies, employees, etc., have the interest in legal entities that produce radio and television programs, so that the membership of such person in the RTM Council could result in a conflict of interest; persons that are sentenced by a final and binding decision, for a criminal offense against official duty, a criminal offense of corruption, fraud, theft or any other criminal offense which makes them unworthy of performing public duty regardless of the sentence imposed or if those persons are sentenced, by final and binding decision, for other criminal offense on sentence of imprisonment exceeding six months, during the period of legal consequences of the sentence; and spouses and persons related to them in the straight line (Article 26 of LPSB).

§3. The Financing of PSB

176. Regional public service broadcasters are funded in variety of ways, via electricity bills, telephone, subscription or taxes with the amount of EUR 3 to EUR 12 per household. For example, Croatia has opted for subscription fees and advertising, Slovenia for subscription, B&H and Macedonia for taxes. Montenegro is the only country who has determined that the public service is financed directly from the budget. In the past, a TV subscription in Montenegro was connected to first the phone bill, and after that to the electricity bill. In the first case, the payment reached barely 60%, and when it stopped, the collection fell to the symbolic 10%. The similar scenario has happened with the electricity bill base. The last Government amendments on the Law on the Public Broadcasting, RTVM receives 0.3% (the previous was 1.2%) of the general budget revenues, but, as explained in the media, this is not a safe model of financing. Under the LPSB, PSB shall be funded from: a part of general incomes of the Budget of Montenegro; production and broadcasting of advertisements; production and sale of audiovisual works (shows, films, series, etc.) and of sound and picture repositories of public interest; sponsorship of program contents; organization of concerts and other manifestations; and the Budget of Montenegro. Although this model is acceptable under EU standards, it has two adversary sides. When the state budget is less, the funds allocated for public service are automatically less. The NGOs often state that by this financing mode, the public service cannot ensure its independency of the broadcast system.

177. The amendments from July 2016 have ensured that the general activities of the RTM shall be funded in the amount of 0.3% of the state budget for the specific year, which is to be transferred monthly, under special instruction. The RTM programs are aimed at broadcasting programs that promote: science and education development; development of culture; and information intended for persons with eyesight and hearing impairments (Article 17 of the LPSB). In addition to this rule, the Law provides that some funds from the budget of Montenegro shall be allocated for programs satisfying citizens' rights. For example, specific funds are allotted for the programs in Albanian and languages of other national and ethnic minorities and these funds cannot be transferred for other purposes.

178. RTM and State (Ministry) shall, within thirty days from the date of coming into effect of the Law on the Budget, contractually regulate mutual rights and liabilities with regard to manner and conditions payment (Article 18).

179. As stated under the Article 19 of the LPSB, "the Budget of Montenegro shall provide the funds for covering the costs of transmission and broadcasting of RTM programs via terrestrial systems, and electronic communications networks without radio frequencies." The payment of the funds from the Budget of Montenegro shall be done in four equal installments. The manner and conditions of providing the funds from the Budget Montenegro shall not influence the editorial independence and autonomy of the RTM. If the budget is not enough to partially cover the costs of transmission and broadcasting of its programs via terrestrial transmission systems and via satellite systems, the RTM shall provide funds.

Chapter 2. Private Broadcasting

§1. Different Categories of Private Broadcasters

180. Under Montenegrin regulation, specifically Article 4 of LEM, an AVM service provider refers to a natural or legal person established in Montenegro with full editorial responsibility for organizing and defining the content of the AVM service. It will be considered established when:

- its head office or residence is in Montenegro and the editorial decisions are taken in Montenegro; or
- its head office or residence is in Montenegro and the editorial decisions are taken in another country, provided that a significant part of the workforce involved in the pursuit of the audiovisual media service activity operates in Montenegro; an AVM service provider has its head office or residence in Montenegro, the editorial decisions are taken in an EU Member State, a significant part of the workforce involved in the pursuit of the audiovisual media service activity operates both in Montenegro and the respective EU Member State; or
- its head office or residence is in Montenegro, the editorial decisions are taken in an EU Member State, a significant part of the workforce involved in the pursuit of the audiovisual media service activity does not operate either in Montenegro or the respective EU Member State, but started media service provision in Montenegro provided that it maintains a stable and effective link with Montenegrin economy; or
- it is established in another country and uses the satellite up-link situated in the territory of Montenegro and/or pertaining to Montenegro, Montenegrin regulation will apply. However, if it is impossible to ascertain whether the AVM service provider falls under the jurisdiction of Montenegro or an EU Member State, the AVM service provider shall fall under the Member State in which it was established in accordance with Articles 52–58 of the Stabilization and Association Agreement between Montenegro and the EU and its Member States.

181. An AVM service provider is obliged to make direct, easy, and permanent access to the recipients of a service regarding the information on: its name, head office, or place of residence, his electronic mail address or website, the competent and its regulatory body.

182. The types of AVM services and their identification process are defined under the Article 46 of LEM. It specifies that an AVM service may be in the form of: electronic media (radio or television broadcasting, electronic publications), on-demand AVM service, and audiovisual commercial communication (ACC). In fact, the Law on Electronic Media provides the clear definition on several categories of the AVM service. At first, it stipulates that an AVM service presents the audiovisual media expression of the editorial program set up with the principal purpose of informing, entertaining, or educating, to the general public by electronic communications networks, and may take the form of electronic media, an on-demand AVM service, ACC (Article 8). Electronic media—a linear AVM service is "a radio or television broadcast which presents a set of information in the form of images and/or sound....constituting an individual item, under the same name, intended to inform and meet the cultural, educational, social and other needs of the public, which enables simultaneous listening to and/or viewing of programmes on the basis of a programme schedule." Montenegrin legal text also provides that on-demand audiovisual service so-called non-linear or encrypted AVM service, is the individual media service which enables the reception of radio and/or television broadcasts. It further states that it functions as "the individual user request and the AVM service provider programmes, available under the contract or other form of authorization." Although the main legal text does not explicitly provide for the private and public broadcasters, it does classify them implicitly in that way by providing that all transmitters of radio and/or television programs can be divided into commercial, non-profit, and public broadcasters. Thus, in the category of private broadcasters there are two types of broadcasters such as: commercial and non-profit broadcasters.

183. The Law on Electronic Media in Article 71 stipulates that commercial broadcasters may produce and broadcast radio and/or television programs in the form of national, regional and local commercial broadcasters. National commercial broadcasters shall cover at least 75% of population in more than ten local self-government units (national coverage or commercial broadcaster network). Regional commercial broadcasters shall cover at least 80% of the population within the territory covering between four and ten local self-government units (regional coverage or commercial broadcaster network). Local commercial broadcasters shall cover at least 85% of the population within the territory covering less than four local self-government units (local coverage or commercial broadcaster network).

184. When granting the broadcasting license, the Council has to determine the status of a non-profit broadcaster. In Article 72 of LEM non-for-profit broadcasters may only be educational establishments, religious, student and non-governmental organizations registered at least three years before applying for acquiring the status of a non-profit broadcaster. In fact, it has to transmit 50% of own production of news daily, cultural, educational, and entertainment programs, with at least 25% of daily production which shall serve the informational, educational, scientific, professional, artistic, cultural, and other needs of the public. The funds for the operation of non-for-profit broadcasters may be raised from donations, contributions of citizens, sponsorships, and other sources of revenues, in accordance with a special law governing the establishment and operation of non-governmental organizations. This category of broadcasters is exempted from payment of the broadcasting license fee. However, the profits gained from radio and/or television program production and transmission can solely be used to improve and develop own activity (Article 72 of LEM).

§2. Licensing Requirements

185. There are several pieces of regulation defining licensing procedure. Along with Part IV of the LEM, Rulebook on Conditions and Procedure of Awarding the Broadcasting Licensing and Rulebook on Awarding Licensing for on-demand AV Media Services, is devoted to the explanation of the licensing procedure. It stipulates that licenses for AVM services provisions shall be granted by the AEM following certain procedure and the criteria. The license shall be granted in the form of: (1) a broadcasting license; and (2) a license for provision of on-demand AVM services. Broadcasting licenses for digital or analog terrestrial, cable, internet, or satellite transmission is to be granted by AEM. It shall be based on: (1) public competitions; and (2) applications for broadcasting license. On the other hand, Internet webcasting shall not be subject to licensing.

186. The procedure of the public competition announcement for granting broadcasting rights (to legal or a natural person intends to broadcast by obtaining access to digital terrestrial broadcasting multiplex) shall be a one-instance administrative procedure, as defined in Article 101 of LEM. The announcement initiated by the AEM's shall be published in the Official Gazette (OG) of Montenegro, on the AEM's website and one daily in Montenegro. Before announcing public competition, the Agency of Electronic Media shall request from the other regulatory body Agency of Electronic Communication and Postal Services the data on availability of frequencies or free resources within digital terrestrial broadcasting multiplex intended for AVM services. The announcement shall contain at least: the scope of public competition (information on the service zone and the pertaining frequencies and/or the number of radio and television programs and the information on the service zone covered by multiplex); selection criteria with scoring methodology; technical requirements for radio and/or television program production and transmission; application fee; amount of deposit; license validity period; application submission deadline etc. (Article 99).

187. The subject of the public competition has to be objective and non-discriminatory and shall refer to: the scope and structure of applicant's programs (diversity, share of own production, European audiovisual works, independent production) and financial data related to the ability for profitable operation and market viability. The applicant offering better guarantees of fostering quality and program diversity shall be given an advantage in the competition process. If an applicant has been already engaged in radio/television broadcasting at the time of public announcement for granting broadcasting rights, the Council is obliged to take into account the contribution of such applicant to the exercise of the principles of professionalism and ethics. The competent authority for granting broadcasting rights is the Council. In the procedure for granting broadcasting rights, the Council shall decide by a written decision, which shall be final. An administrative dispute may be instigated against the decision. The Council is obliged: (1) to post on AEM's website the list of applicant s with orderly and timely applications; (2) dismiss incomplete and untimely applications; (3) pass the decision on granting broadcasting rights; (4) publicly announce the decision as per the competition, in appropriate way. Once public competition for granting broadcasting rights is finalized, AEM director is obliged to: publicly announce the list of persons being granted broadcasting license; and, submit to the Agency for electronic communication a copy of the broadcasting license issued (Articles 100–101 of LEM).

188. Montenegrin law provides that the procedure for granting licenses for on-demand broadcasting can be initiated by: (1) public broadcaster; (2) a legal or a natural person registered with the competent authority, or with the competent court, for pursuing the activity of radio or television broadcasting. Law provides that applicants shall submit: registration evidence; a certified copy of the Memorandum and the Articles of Association; an organizational chart and job systematization; a program with the data on the scope and structure of programs (diversity, a share of own production, of European audiovisual works, of independent production) and the identification sign; proof of no pending proceedings before the competent court, or the responsible person within the applicant for misuse of official authorities or economic crimes or for offenses punishable by imprisonment etc. (Article 102). This application shall be decided upon by the AEM Director within fifteen days. The decision may be appealed against before Council. The Council's decision shall be final and contestable by an administrative dispute.

189. A broadcasting license issued under the public competition procedure and the application for granting broadcasting licenses shall, *inter alia,* contain the information on: "the license holder; the name of the radio or television program; the program structure and other program requirements in terms with the application filed per the public competition or the request for granting the license; type of electronic communication networks for distribution of radio and/or television program; radio frequencies granted as per the public competition, when analog broadcasting systems are used for provision of AVM service of radio and/or television broadcasts; access of AVM service providers to movable capacities of separate radio or television programs within a multiplex, when digital broadcasting systems are used for provision of AVM service of radio and/ or television broadcasts; identification sign of the radio or television program; deadline for commencing broadcasting; license validity period; fee amount and payment modalities; other rights and obligations of license holders" (Article 104 of LEM). Broadcasting license may not, on temporary or permanent basis, be assigned, leased or otherwise transferred without Council's approval. A political party, organization, or coalition, or a legal entity founded by a political party, organization, or coalition may not be a broadcaster (Article 104 LEM).

190. A person who has not acquired the right to broadcast shall be refunded the deposit paid within seven days from issuance of the final decision. For those who have acquired the right to broadcast, the deposit amount shall be factored into the broadcasting fee amount. The deposit is not refundable to the broadcasting license holder who: before commencing broadcasting, notifies the AEM that they would not broadcast or use radio frequency granted as per the license; fails to commence broadcasting within the time stipulated (Article 106 LEM)

191. Broadcasting licenses shall be issued for the period of fifteen years. For the sake of timely switchover from analog to digital terrestrial broadcasting systems, the license may be granted with shorter validity period, which may not be shorter than two years. The license is renewable if the license holder files a license renewal request with the AEM not later than six months before the expiry of the current license. Article 109 further states: "when the broadcasting license was granted as per the public competition, taking into account the conduct of the license holder for the period of license validity, following the public competition the AEM: shall grant the license renewal, with the current license holder being giving precedence providing he meets the public competition requirements."

192. The Law provides that the broadcasting license can cease to be valid in two ways: voluntarily and forcefully. The broadcasting license shall cease to be valid: with the expiry of the time period to which it was granted; upon the written request of the license holder; by revoking the license; in case of broadcaster's liquidation (Article 109 of LEM). The AEM director shall revoke the license in several situations prescribed by the LEM. As provided under the Article 110 of LEM, a failure to: pay the fee, rectify the irregularities regarding unlawful media concentration, submit correct data or data relevant for decision-making in the license application process, to broadcast within the time period cited in the license. In addition to it, if broadcaster was pronounced on two consecutive occasions the measure of temporary revocation of license or the broadcaster interrupts broadcasting for more than ten days in a row or fifteen days with interruptions within one calendar year the Agency may revoke the license. This decision may be appealed before the Council within fifteen days from the day of the decision delivery, and the same timeframe is determined for the Council to decide. This Council's decision shall be final and may be contested in administrative dispute proceedings (Articles 109–110).

193. The provisions governing the procedure for granting and revocation of broadcasting license shall apply mutatis mutandis to the procedure for granting and revoking the license for provision of on-demand AVM services (Article 116). However, this procedure is also defines under the Article 116 of LEM. This Article states that a license for provision of on-demand AVM services shall be obtained based on: "(1) a public competition, when the on-demand AVM service provider intends to use terrestrial radio frequencies for provision of AVM services; (2) a request, when the on-demand AVM service provider intends to use electronic communications networks for the provision of AVM service without relying on terrestrial broadcasting frequencies." Before public competition, AEM is obliged to obtain from the Agency for Electronic Communications and Postal Services (AECPS), data on available frequencies or available capacities on digital terrestrial broadcasting multiplex intended for AVM services. Contents of the public competition for the provision of on-demand AVM services are defined under the Article 117. In fact, it states that public competition for provision of AVM services shall contain: information on radio frequencies offered at the public competition and intended for use by on-demand AVM service providers; information on the envisaged number of radio and television programs for which the right to access digital broadcasting multiplex is granted via the public competition; eligibility criteria; criteria with methodology; fee; amount of deposit which may not exceed one quarter of annual fee for provision of on-demand AVM services; license validity period; application submission deadline (not be shorter than thirty days from the public announcement); deadline for decision (not be longer than sixty days from the expiry of the application submission deadline); list of supporting documents (Article 117).

194. The selection criteria shall be objective and referring to: scope and structure of applicant's program package that the on-demand AVM service provider intends to distribute; financial data related to ability for profitable operation and market viability. Under Article 118 of LEM, the license for provision of on-demand AVM services shall contain the data on: the name of the license holder and of the on-demand AVM service; service zone; catalog of programs and other contents; annual fee and payment modalities; license validity period; deadline for commencing broadcasting; other rights and obligations of the license holder. The license may not be assigned, leased or otherwise transferred without Council's approval (Article 118).

195. An on-demand AVM service provider is obliged, within time limit, to furnish to AEM: a contract concluded with the operator of at least one such network; proof of entry into the Register of Operators maintained by the AECPS. Any contract with operators of electronic communications networks concluded after the expiry of the deadline shall be also furnished to AEM. An on-demand AVM service provider is obliged to enter into a (sub) contract with the end user governing the manner and terms of provision of the service of radio and television program distribution and other on-demand AVM services. This contract shall contain in particular the provisions on: access fee amount and payment modality; monthly fee amount and payment modality; catalog of programs included in the distribution service; terms and procedure for filing a complaint related to the work of an on-demand AVM service provider (Article 121).

196. AEM shall keep a register of licenses for AVM providers (Article 127). Agency Council has the right to determine method of keeping a register. Furthermore, it is also obliged to provide to the state administration authority responsible for media the data from the register.

Chapter 3. Program Standards

197. In the programs of the electronic media, the media is obliged to consistently apply professional and ethical standards of journalists' code of conduct, and appropriately inform the public, expressing compassion and eliminating any risk of sensationalism. Along with the standards for media outlet regulated in the bylaws—Media Law and Law on Electronic Media, Rulebook on Programme Standards in the Electronic Media (RPSEM) is the relevant legislative piece defining these issues. Rulebook on Programme Standards in Electronic Media (RPSEM) provides for the general and special program standards. Within the general standards, the Rulebook defines the principles of freedom and accountability, whereas the special program rules discuss: protection of privacy, prohibition of hate speech, protection of minors, respect of court and secrecy of proceedings, religion in the electronic media programs and related parapsychology, quackery and fortune telling, language and linguistic rules in the electronic media programs etc.

198. The principal criteria to determine the quality of the program standards are: truthfulness, sincerity, balanced reporting, objectivity, and impartiality. A broadcasting license holder may be a legal or a natural person registered with the competent authority. In order to be registered an AVM service provider shall meet special technical, office and staff requirements for radio and television program production and broadcasting. Compliance with the requirements—program-related obligations of broadcasters shall be verified during regular inspection supervision, following granting of a broadcasting license (Article 55). A broadcaster shall ensure the adherence to the following principles: "(1) free, true, integral, impartial, and timely information of the public of events in the country and abroad; (2) respect and promote democratic values, institutions, and pluralism of ideas; (3) foster culture of public dialogue and respect for linguistic standards; (4) preservation of cultural assets; (5) fundamental human rights and freedoms, especially the privacy and dignity of citizens and protection of minors" (Article 55(6)).

199. The general television or radio broadcasting program shall provide the information on: type of program, or specific groups; envisaged shares of specific program groups; projection of the maximum share of advertising contents; envisaged share of own audiovisual works; transmission time (Article 56). Furthermore, this Article states that the program base of a specialized television or radio broadcast shall convey: program type, of which over 50% shall be programs of the same type; proportions of different types of programs; maximum share of advertising; share of European audiovisual production and other works for specialized television broadcasting; transmission time. A significant change (over 10% in the program structure) in the structure of a radio or television broadcast shall be accompanied with the AEM's approval (Article 58). AEM may deny the change "should it determine that it would lead in the area covered by a certain radio or television broadcast to a lack of a certain type of programmes for which the broadcaster was licensed to use frequencies which by the Radio Frequency Allocation Plan were envisaged for analogue broadcasting or in case of acquiring the right of access to multiplex for digital terrestrial broadcasting" (Article 56).

200. In accordance with the Law, Rulebooks on Programme Standards in Electronic Media (RPSEM) promote fair, adequate, balanced reporting, which can be achieved by respecting the principle *audiatur et altera pars* and thereby providing both-conflicting opinions. Program shall not tendentiously promote the interests of any group or individual. In fact, journalists, editors can freely express their views on the certain topics; however, they have to make sure that the audience recognizes them as such. Otherwise, it will be treated as the abuse which leads to distribution and infringement of impartiality and balanced reporting.

201. The Rulebook on the Programme Standards in Electronic Media, classifies program standards into the principles stating positive and negative obligation of the broadcaster. More succinctly, all program standards are divided into two categories: general and specific standards listed in the Articles 5–45. General program standards are defined in the three categories: (1) Freedom and accountability, (2) Prohibited programs, and (3) News programs. Special program standards include: (1) Protection of privacy, (2) Offensive language and hate speech, (3) Protection of Minors, (4) Written and acoustic warning and graphical signs, (5) Respect of court and secrecy of proceedings, (6) Religion in the electronic media programs, (7) Parapsychology, quackery, and fortunetelling, (8) Language and linguistic rules in the electronic media programs, (9) The participation of audience in the electronic media programs, (10) Repeat programs and archive materials. Out of these principles, there are nine standing out as most relevant once. These are: (1) prohibition of violation of human dignity; (2) freedom of advertising and sponsorship; (3) accuracy, completeness in reporting; (4) recognizability of advertisers and sponsors; (5) prohibition of abuse of confidence; (6) prohibition of discrimination; (7) prohibition of violation of morals; (8) protection of minors' rights; (9) respect and protection of competition. The Agency of Electronic Media, as main media regulator, has the obligation to occasionally conduct the research on implementation of these standards. In fact, conducted monitoring has the aim to determine the implementation of the regulation on program standards stipulated in the Law on Electronic Media, and Rules on program standards in electronic media outlets. As an example of these mandatory activities we provide the research that Agency conducting via monitored broadcasted program for a period of seven days, from November 5 to 11, 2015 from 6 p.m. to 12 p.m. The monitoring has been conducted on the programs of the one public broadcaster TVM, and four private commercial broadcasters such as TV Vijesti, TV Prva, TV PINK, and TV Atlas.[112]

§1. Impartiality

202. The Law on Electronic Media provides the general guiding rules on ensuring free, true, integral, impartial, and timely dissemination of information. Radio or television outlets shall realistically present the events/topics with variety of adequately presented approaches and opinions: News shall truly and professionally, accurately, and impartially present facts and events; opinions and comments shall be separated

112. Agency of Electronic Media, Report on the Application of the Programme of super works Standards in Audio-Visual Communications in Electronic Media, January 2016, available at: http://www.ardcg.org/index.php?option=com_docman&task=cat_view&gid=43&Itemid=26).

and their source or author recognizable; impartiality shall be encouraged, respecting the difference of opinion on political or economic matters. The audience shall be provided with the accurate, unambiguous, non-exaggerated information, and realistic view on the events/topics. Accordingly, principle of impartiality has to be encouraged via the standard of clear separation of factual reporting from "the positions, opinions or comments, not allowing the personal convictions and opinions of editors and journalist to have a discriminatory effect on the selection of subject and the manner of its presentation" (Article 4 of the RPSEM).

203. The misuse and misrepresentation of "statements, press releases, and similar contents, aimed at changing their actual meaning or manipulation with images, tone or contents distorting the original meaning of the statement" shall be sanctioned and strongly prohibited. The principle of impartiality is intrinsically linked with the principle of objectivity and principle of accuracy. The meaning and content of both are strictly defined under the RPSEM, so that an obligation of the media "to present all points of view in their news programmes, in an objective manner, without editorial interventions and comments favoring anybody" has been determined as the principle of objectivity. In the same manner, the Rules provide the obligation of media outlet to accurately report so that they have "to relay on the facts in their reporting" and try to avoid broadcast "of the news and reports they know or could know to be inaccurate." In fact, it is stated that "news and reports that could not be verified, or whose accuracy has not been established with certainty, may be broadcast only if they are clearly identified as unofficial or unconfirmed."

204. The strong need for the application and adherence to these principles has been determined during the election campaign process. Balanced and fair reporting, adherence to the principle of *audiatur et altera pars*, publishing conflicting opinions on controversial political, economic, and other topics of public interest shall be the main features of media reporting through the election campaigns process. The Rules strictly determine the obligation of the electronic media to refrain from tendentious "promotion of the interests of a political party of any group or individual, especially if such content is broadcast repeatedly over a certain period." It further states that media anchors, reporters, authors of the programs, moderators in news, political and current affairs programs, debates and discussions, may express their personal views and opinions on, which must be clearly identified, enabling the audience to recognize them as such. Journalists are expected to impartially disseminate information, without expressing personal views, in any verbal or non-verbal way. Their roles within the programs shall not be seen as the promotion of the views of one political actors or interest groups (Article 6 of Rules).

§2. Cultural Diversity

205. The promotion of fundamental human rights and freedoms, democratic values, and pluralism of ideas and media outlets, culture of public dialogue assumes free, correct, complete, impartial, and timely dissemination of information to the public. Cultural diversity has been seen as a significant part of Montenegrin tradition. It also has been embodied in several legal acts starting with the Constitution. Article 78 of the Constitution has declared the duty to develop a spirit of mutual respect. It precisely defines the duty of everyone in the field of education, culture, media, and public life to promote and develop the spirit of tolerance, mutual respect, and cooperation among people regardless of their ethnic, cultural, linguistic, and religious identity.

206. Cultural diversity is dealt with in both Media Law and Law on Electronic Media. Under Article 55 of ML, a broadcaster is obliged to store transmitted programs in line with regulations governing media and preservation of cultural assets. A broadcaster is obliged to foster culture of public dialogue and respect for linguistic standards.

207. Broadcasters are obliged to transmit radio or television programs in Montenegrin language, in Latin or Cyrillic script, or in other languages in official use. The use of Montenegrin language is not mandatory in case of: (1) showing films and other audio and audiovisual works in their original form; (2) showing works of music with lyrics partly or wholly in a foreign language; (3) programs partly or fully intended for study of a foreign language and script. The use of Montenegrin language is not mandatory in programs intended for members of minority nations and other minority communities (Article 57 of LEM).

208. Religion in electronic media programs, as defined in the Articles 32–33 has been strongly protected in the Rulebook on Programme Standards in Electronic Media, by stating that media programs shall not abuse religion, faith, or denomination. It further emphasizes that programs related to religion, faith, or denomination shall be accompanied with the accurate and objective religious communities. The electronic media shall not report in an influential manner so as to try to change audience's faith or religious beliefs. The broadcasters are obliged to clearly announce religious programs and make clear which religion/church or religious community is in question. All programs dedicated to paranormal, quackery, fortune telling, parapsychological, and occultism phenomena shall not be broadcast outside the watershed (Article 34 of the RSPEL). On the other hand, the entertainment programs with the astrological predictions, interpretation of horoscopes or similar content, may be broadcast outside the watershed, if they are not the only content of the program and if there is no participation of the audience.

209. Regarding the language and linguistic rules in the electronic media programs, it states that broadcasters are obliged to pay attention to the language used in the public sphere, to its ethical and political correctness, as well as to its grammatical accuracy (Articles 38–41 of the RSPEL). The electronic media are obliged to broadcast radio and television programs in the Montenegrin language, in Latin or Cyrillic script, or another language in official use, in compliance with the Constitution of Montenegro and the Electronic Media Law. The public service broadcasters, especially the national public broadcasting service, have a legal obligation to promote and cherish the Montenegrin national and cultural identity and the Montenegrin cultural heritage, and are obliged to make sure that their production includes the highest possible share of programs in the Montenegrin language, and to have adequate use of the Montenegrin Language in the translated programs. The broadcasters are obliged to provide an adequate use of the Montenegrin language in the programs they produced and in the translation (subtitling and dubbing) of all programs produced in the languages that are not in the official use in Montenegro, which requires a simple voiceover, without any need for a creative interpretation of characters by actors. The broadcasters are obliged to make sure that the language in the broadcast program is grammatically accurate, unless it is used in the dramaturgic or artistic context. However, news, education, and similar programs are limited with respect to the type of language used, so that swearing, derogatory language, vulgarities, and jargon are forbidden. The public service broadcasters are obliged to ensure an overall quality of expression of newsreaders and reporters, including professional editing of the materials before broadcasting.

§3. Protection of Minors

210. The rights of media, freedom of the press are paramount concerns when minors are involved. The analyses have shown that there is often a clash between the rights of the minors to confidentiality and protection of their best interests and the right of the media to access of information.[113] When the rights of two interest groups such as the press and the juvenile offender come into conflict, the courts and the legal community are tasked with providing a framework for resolution. However, in countries that have only recently recognized the right of free press and free speech, there is the problem that these rights will be practiced in excess or even abused to the detriment of other conflicting rights such as the individual right to privacy. When seen and analyzed through the lenses of the most susceptible, social vulnerable group—minors—the conflict between these two rights must be more strictly scrutinized.[114]

211. Minors are strongly protected in a number of international instruments relevant for Montenegrin national system on an obligatory or voluntary basis.

212. The UN Convention on the Rights of the Child[115] ratified and thereby incorporated in Montenegrin legal system strongly protects the interests and rights of child, so it states that all actions concerning children shall be conducted in the best interests of the child (Article 3). Furthermore, it states that "a child shall not be subjected to arbitrary or unlawful interference with his or her privacy, family, or correspondence, nor to unlawful attacks on his or her honour and reputation and that the child has the right to the protection of the law against any interference" (Article 16). Along the UN Convention on the Rights of the Child 1989, there are some other international relevant legal instruments providing for children's access to justice at international level, such as: Article 6 of the European Convention, Article 14(4) International Covenant On

113. Spaić, A., Nolasco, C., *Mediji i djeca u SAD-u, UNAPREĐIVANJE MEDIJSKIH PRAVA, Fakultet političkih nauka*, Podgorica, 2013, pp. 99–109, ISBN 978-9940-9102-5-9; Đuranović, D., *Osvrt na medijsko izvještavanje o maloljetnicima: Sukob etike i profita, UNAPREĐIVANJE MEDIJSKIH PRAVA, Fakultet političkih nauka*, Podgorica, 2013, pp. 48–56, ISBN 978-9940-9102-5-9; Maric, B., *Maloljetnici, postupak, javnost, UNAPREĐIVANJE MEDIJSKIH PRAVA, Fakultet političkih nauka*, Podgorica, 2013, pp. 40–48, ISBN 978-9940-9102-5-9; Sekulovic, S., *Preispitivanje postojeceg zakonskog okvira izvjestavanja o maloljetnicima, UNAPREĐIVANJE MEDIJSKIH PRAVA, Fakultet političkih nauka*, Podgorica, 2013, pp. 30–40, ISBN 978-9940-9102-5-9.

114. Nolasco, C., Spaic, A., Vaughn, M.S., *Media Access to Juvenile Proceedings: Balancing the Tightrope Between Privacy Rights and Freedom of the Press*, 43 Int'l J.L, Crime & Just. 4, 643–675.

115. The UN Convention on the Rights of the Child 1989 was adopted by the General Assembly of the UN on Nov. 20, 1989.

Civil And Political Rights 1966 (ICCPR) and Convention on the Protection of Children Against Sexual Exploitation and Sexual Abuse.[116] International Covenant on Civil and Political Rights stipulates that: "In the case of juvenile persons, the procedure shall take account of their age and the desirability of promoting their rehabilitation." Furthermore, the Convention on the Protection of Children Against Sexual Exploitation and Sexual Abuse states that: "Each party shall take the necessary legislative or other measures to protect the rights and interests of victims, including their special needs as witnesses ... Protecting their privacy, their identity and their image;" (Article 31).[117] Also, its Explanatory Report, in paragraph 222 discusses the protection of the victim-child's identity, image and privacy.

213. There is also the Council of Europe Strategy on the Rights of the Child 2012–2015 and Guidelines of the Committee of Ministers of the Council of Europe on child-friendly justice and their explanatory memorandum and The Beijing Rules—the United Nations Standard Minimum Rules for the Administration of Juvenile Justice.[118] The Beijing Rules, although not binding rules in international law, adopted by the United Nations General Assembly in 1985, in Article 8, paragraph 1 stipulate that: "(t)he juvenile's privacy shall be respected at all stages in order to avoid harm being caused to her or him by undue publicity or by the process of labeling. Furthermore, the paragraph 2 of the same article states that, '(i) ... no information that may lead to the identification of a juvenile offender shall be published'. Furthermore, Article 17 of the same text, stipulates that the reaction shall be proportional to the gravity of the offense ... The well-being of the juvenile shall be the guiding factor in the consideration of her or his case."

214. Also, there are the Guidelines of the Committee of Ministers of the Council of Europe on child-friendly justice and their explanatory memorandum, providing that the privacy, personal data, and all other information on children who involved in judicial proceedings shall enjoy strong protection. This implies that no information or personal data may be made available or published, particularly in the media, which

116. European Convention on Human Rights and Fundamental Freedoms, available at http://www.echr.coe.int/Documents/Convention_ENG.pdf; International Covenant On Civil And Political Rights (ICCPR) *adopted by the United Nations General Assembly on 16 December* 1966, available at https://treaties.un.org/doc/publication/unts/volume%20999/volume-999-i-14668-english.pdf; Council of Europe Convention on the Protection of Children against Sexual Exploitation and Sexual Abuse, July 12, 2007, CETS No: 201, available at https://www.coe.int/en/web/conventions/full-list/-/conventions/treaty/201.

117. Council of Europe Convention on the Protection of Children Against Sexual Exploitation and Sexual Abuse (General measures of protection) of October 25, 2007, CETS No. 201.

118. Council of Europe Strategy on the Rights of the Child 2012–2015, CM(2011)171 final, available at http://www.coe.int/t/DGHL/STANDARDSETTING/CDcj/StrategyCME.pdf; Guidelines of the Committee of Ministers of the Council of Europe on child-friendly justice and their explanatory memorandum (Adopted by the Committee of Ministers on November 17, 2010 at the 1098th meeting of the Ministers' Deputies Guidelines and Explanatory memorandum – version edited May 31, 2011, available at: http://www.coe.int/t/dghl/standardsetting/childjustice/Guidelines%20on%20child-friendly%20justice%20and%20their%20explanatory%20memorandum%20_4_.pdf; The Beijing Rules - the United Nations Standard Minimum Rules for the Administration of Juvenile Justice, adopted by General Assembly resolution 40/33 of November 29, 1985, available at http://www.ohchr.org/Documents/ProfessionalInterest/beijingrules.pdf.

could disclose child's identity via image, description of family members, addresses, etc. Also, Member States shall determine limited access to all documents and data with personal and sensitive data of children. In all judicial and other interventions, children should be protected from harm, intimidation, and reprisals.[119]

215. It also seems relevant to mention the most relevant legal texts without compulsory effects: Recommendation Rec (85)11 (Recommendation No. Rec (85)11 adopted by Committee of Ministers of the Council of Europe on June 28, 1985) dealing with "the position of the victim in the framework of criminal law and procedure." Recommendations No. Rec (87)20 stipulating "that social reactions to juvenile delinquency should take account of the personality and specific needs of minors, and that the latter need specialized interventions and, where appropriate, specialized treatment." There are two relevant recommendations that have been implemented in the Montenegrin legal system. These are: Recommendation Rec (2001)16 on the protection of children against sexual exploitation (Recommendation Rec (2001)16 adopted on October 31, 2001 the Committee of Ministers of the Council of Europe) and Recommendation Rec (2003)13 providing for the Protection of privacy of minors or other vulnerable persons during ongoing criminal proceedings (Recommendation Rec (2003)13 adopted on July 10, 2003 the Committee of Ministers of the Council of Europe).

216. In accordance with the European Convention on Human Rights, the vital interest of any society assumes fair trial without intimidation and victimization of the child. Accordingly, ECtHR in the most recent *Krone Verlag GmbH v. Austria, ECtHR Judgement* (June 19, 2012) Application No. 27306/07, attempted to establish a future pattern for media access to juvenile proceedings within a broader legal framework that will result in a more standard and uniform application across European nations. Furthermore, this case increases current knowledge of the legal standards and framework for media coverage of juvenile offenders, as the part of the higher education of journalists, dealing and reporting on the juvenile proceedings, judges who are expected to be familiar with the international standards and the practice of European Court of Human Rights. The analysis in this article aims to increase awareness of the boundaries of media role in treating juveniles, and to improve consistency in media access to juvenile proceedings by taking into consideration the findings of the cases before European Court of Human Right.[120]

217. In the same manner as the international legal community, the national legislator has ensured the protection of minors. Article 74 of the Constitution specifies the content of the rights of a child. It provides that children shall enjoy human rights appropriate to their age and maturity and to preserve their identity. Special protection of children from mental, physical, social, economic, and any other exploitation or abuse shall be guaranteed. In fact, the interests of a child shall be the primary focus

119. Guidelines of the Committee of Ministers of the Council of Europe on child-friendly justice and their explanatory memorandum (Adopted by the Committee of Ministers on November 17, 2010 at the 1098th meeting of the Ministers' Deputies Guidelines and Explanatory memorandum - version edited May 31, 2011, available at: http://www.coe.int/t/dghl/standardsetting/childjustice/Guidelines%20on%20child-friendly%20justice%20and%20their%20explanatory%20memorandum%20_4_.pdf.

120. Spaic, A., et al., Krone case, *supra.*, p. 12.

of public authorities, state or private institutions, especially in the area of children's protection in the area of freedom of expressions, in accordance with their age and maturity. The procedure and manner of child protection is determined in several laws: Constitution, Media Law, Law on Electronic Media, Criminal Code etc.

218. As stated under the *legi generali,* i.e., the Media Law (ML), Article 22 states that media shall protect the integrity of minors. Any programming that could endanger the health, moral, intellectual, emotional, and social development of a child shall clearly and visibly be marked beforehand as such and distributed in a way with the least possibility for a child to use it. It is also forbidden to publicize the identity of a minor involved in a criminal act, either in the capacity of a victim or a defendant. As an exception to it, the identity of a minor, sentenced for a criminal offense by a final judgment, may be publicized if there is an overriding interest of the public to be informed.

219. In the same manner, Article 55 of the Law on Electronic Media (LEM) defines that a broadcaster is obliged to protect the integrity of minors by publishing audio and visual warning for programs which may impair the physical health, moral, mental, intellectual, emotional, and social development of minors and clearly identify such programs by the presence of a visual symbol throughout their duration and to broadcast such programs at a time and in a manner in which it is least likely that minors will normally hear or see it.

220. The ACC shall not: cause tangible or intangible detriment to minors; directly exhort minors to buy or hire a product or a service by exploiting their inexperience or credulity; directly encourage minors to persuade their parents or others to purchase the goods or services being advertised; exploit the special trust minors place in parents, teachers, or other persons; unreasonably show minors in dangerous situations. ACC for alcoholic beverages shall not be aimed at minors and shall not encourage consumption of such beverages (Articles 85 and 86). Also Article 82, defines that an on-demand AVM service provider shall ensure that services which may impair the physical or mental development of minors will not normally be heard or seen.

221. The Rulebook on the Programme Standards of the Electronic Media (RPSEM) are also very strict, and extensive providing for the precise and detailed list of the recommendations regarding the protection of this group. Article 19 of the RPSEM specifies that in the television broadcasting, there is a watershed between midnight and 6 a.m. The programs intended for adults only, which could have detrimental effect or consequences for the minors, shall be broadcast only within the watershed. It specifies further in Article 20, that the information on any form of violence and the related role of minors, the identity of minors shall always be protected by scrambled or blurred image and modulated tone, making them unrecognizable. Personal data of minors and details from their family relations and private life shall not be published in the cases when it could result in the violation of their interests or dignity. Also, the information on the ongoing criminal proceedings against minors and the related court decisions shall not be published. A binding court decision in the proceedings against minors can be published, without providing their personal data or other information on the basis of which their identity could be established. When publishing information related to criminal cases, the electronic media are obliged to pay special attention to the vulnerable position of minors involved in these cases, either as a victims, witnesses, or perpetrators.

Identity of a minor convicted of a crime by a binding decision may be revealed in the program only if there is an overriding public interest. Article 21 defines that minors are allowed to directly participate in the programs only with prior written consent of their parents, guardians, custodians, stepparents, or persons in charge of their care, education, or training. As an exception, minors may participate in the news and entertainment programs without prior consent of the relevant persons only if it is necessary for the timely coverage of the topical issues. Regardless of the consent, the minors shall not be insulted or disrespected in any way. Entertainment programs shall not use family conflicts to entertain the audience, impairing the development of children in that way. The prizes awarded to minors shall correspond to their age. Direct participation of minors in the programs shall not provoke anxiety or fear of the minors, or impair their physical, mental, or emotional well-being and dignity. The electronic media shall not solicit the opinion of the minors, related to the private family matters or topics that can be beyond their understanding. Minors shall not participate in programs that include discussions about the adequacy of their custody with one parent or the other, acceptability of their departure from home, living with a foster family, or adoption, or the harm caused by the behavior of either of the parents. Minors shall not be used for political purposes. Furthermore, Article 22 states that the electronic media are obliged to provide prior acoustic and visual (written and graphic) identification of the programs that could impair the physical condition, health, moral, mental, intellectual, emotional, and social development of minors. The programs shall be clearly identified by a visual symbol throughout the program, and broadcast at the time and in the way least likely for minors to watch or listen to in normal circumstances. Minors shall not be carelessly and unreasonably shown in dangerous situations. Minors in crisis situations shall not be interviewed (e.g., children who ran away from home, attempted suicide, used by the adults to commit a crime, whose parents are serving a prison sentence, etc.) and their anonymity shall be ensured in the coverage of these situations. The parts of news programs that could impair the physical, mental, or moral development of minors shall be announced by a warning that disturbing or violent scenes are to follow. The consumption of tobacco or tobacco products, alcohol, and narcotics shall not be shown in the programs targeting primarily minors, except if they are identified as harmful. All forms of violence or dangerous behavior easily imitable by minors shall not be portrayed in the programs targeting primarily minors, except if they are identified as harmful. Articles 23–27 of RSPEM specify that warning and graphical signs shall immediately precede the identified program, with the following text: The following program is not suitable for minors under the age of 16 or 18, simultaneously read by a presenter. For the purpose of this Rulebook, the following graphical signs shall be used for adequate programs: (1) graphical sign 16; and (2) graphical sign 18. The graphical sign 16, identifies the content, aired between 10 p.m. and 6 a.m., not suitable for the minors under the age of 16, *inter alia,* including: the scenes of violence and its after-effects, portrayal of injuries, wounds and blood, nudity and sexuality, portrayal of a sexual intercourse, use of vulgar and offensive language The programs with the graphical sign 18 shall be broadcast between midnight and 6 a.m. only (Articles 21–27).

222. The Codex of Montenegrin Ethics 2016 specifies that "a journalist is obliged to protect the integrity of minors." In the Guidelines, the children's interest is ensured by providing that media is obliged to comply with the principles of the UN Convention on the Rights of Children and to research with special care the information that affect children's interests and to exercise special sympathy when interviewing, photographing, or filming children under the age of sixteen.

§4. Human Dignity

223. Montenegrin warfare tradition and history has been grounded in the ethical value of "Humanity and Bravery" permeated with dignity, self-sacrifice for the just cause, and respect for others. Ever since human dignity has been strongly present, not only in the written but also unwritten part of Montenegrin cultural, social, and legal heritage. As such, it has been incorporated in the laws proclaiming that freedom of speech and human dignity are the democratic values of the equal constitutional strength.

224. Along with the protection of human dignity in the international treaties such as the European Convention, Article 10 paragraph 2, several Montenegrin legal text explicitly provides the protection of the democratic value in the context of protecting freedom of expression. Freedom of expression may be subject to formalities, conditions, restrictions, or penalties, necessary in a democratic society, *inter alia,* for the protection of the reputation or rights of others.

225. In the same context, Constitution of Montenegro, in Article 49(2) provides for the implicit protection of the human dignity by proclaiming that right to freedom of expression shall be deemed to be abused if used to violate dignity, reputation and honor of others, public morality, to endanger the state or its security, and to damage the authority of the court without grounds.

226. Article 20 of the Media Law stipulates that an establishing founder shall be accountable for every published programming. If a medium publicizes the programming that violates and insults the honor of the individual, gives or conveys untrue statements about his life, knowledge and abilities, or insults his dignity in any other way, the person interested shall have the right to press legal charges with the competent court against the author and founder of the medium for the compensation of damage. Article 55 of the Law on Electronic Media further states that a broadcaster is obliged to respect the dignity of citizens. It further states that the media outlet is obliged to not only respect it but to contribute to its further protection and promotion as a fundamental human right and democratic value.

227. The Law on Contracts and Torts in Article 151 states that whoever insults another person's honor, although being aware, or should have to be aware that these are damaging materials to that person, shall be liable for damages. However, the law further states that no one shall be liable for the loss caused when insulting another person's dignity without knowing it, should they or the one acknowledging the statement have a serious interest in the matter.

228. The Rules on the Programme Standards in Electronic Media, in Article 5, determine that audiovisual commercial service shall be *inter alia,* and based on prohibition of violation of human dignity. It further specifies that "audiovisual commercial communication shall not prejudice respect for human dignity" (Article 5 RPSEM).

229. Guidelines of the Codex of Montenegrin Journalists, 2016 explicitly states that a journalist is obliged to respect human dignity. In another manner, more implicitly, principle 10 of the Codex proclaims the presumption of innocence and thus protects human dignity. It states that prejudicial portrayals and allegations violate the constitutional protection of human dignity. Furthermore, throughout the text of the Guidelines, it protects this value of the modern society. For example, it provides that while interviewing, the journalist has to demonstrate care which must be taken to protect the interviewee against any distortions or impairments, which may jeopardize his or her dignity or legitimate interests.

§5. Right to Reply

230. As already stipulated,[121] the right to reply presents one of the most effective and most used instruments of the injured party. As such it has been recognized in a number of national legal texts. The Constitution of Montenegro recognizes and defines the right to reply and the right to a correction. It states that the right to reply and correct any untrue, incomplete or incorrectly conveyed information which violates a person's right or interest and the right to compensation of damage caused by the publication of untruthful data or information shall be guaranteed in the Montenegrin national system (Article 49 paragraph 2). Accordingly, the whole set of national legal instruments have set this right to reply.

231. The Criminal Code in Article 180 states the crime on prevention of publication of responses and rectifications. In fact, it states that "anyone who, contrary to the final decision by a court of law, rejects or prevents to publicize a response or rectification of an incorrectly published information which violates someone's rights or interests, shall be sentenced to a fine or imprisonment not exceeding one year" (Article 180 PC).

232. Law on Electronic Media (LEM) and Media Law (ML) define it in the same manner, since LEM, in Article 47, directed the reader to the application of the general rules on right to reply determined in ML. The right to reply is defined in Media law in the Articles 26–35. It states that a reply presents any information which denies or corrects statements in the published program. A person whose constitutional rights have been violated is entitled to a right to reply, free of charge. Right to reply assumes the fulfillment of the following two conditions: (1) it has to be requested not later than thirty days from the day of publishing the programming; (2) it shall be stated which programming the reply refers to. The reply shall be broadcasted or in the first or the second subsequent broadcast media programming, without any modification, and in proportional length of the programming. As specified under Article 26, the targeted media is obliged to broadcast a reply, unless: "a reply does not refer to the programming which was the reason for claiming their publishing or does not contain actual data referring to the claims published in the programming; a reply denies the content of a published programming whose authenticity was verified by a valid decision of a competent authority; a reply was submitted by a person the programming does not refer to; a reply to the same programming has already been published at the request of the authorized person or the reaction of the authorized person of the same content as the submitted correction or reply has already been published in the same medium,

121. The legislative framework on right to reply has been covered in Chapter 4 in paras (122–129).

in some other equally valid form (interview, statement, etc.); reply to the same programme was submitted, with the same content as the earlier one, and the proceedings with regard to publishing of the earlier submitted correction or reply is not finished; reply does not refer to the programming, which the person claims to be correcting or replying to; reply is such that its publishing would result in medium distribution banning,[122] criminal or penal accountability, or civil legal accountability toward third persons, reply was not signed by a person authorized by a legal person or if a natural person who submitted reply failed to write his identity card number and residential address on it, reply disproportionately exceeds the length of a related programming and a submitter thereof rejects the written claim of editor-in-chief of the medium requesting appropriate shortening of the reply" (Article 26 ML).

233. However, if a broadcaster rejects to act accordingly and publish the reply, a lawsuit can be initiated before competent court. In fact, not later than thirty days from the deadline set for publishing reply, the complaint shall be filed against the founder of the medium, together with the contested piece. Once the lawsuit is filed, the media is requested to submit sound or video recording of the programming in order to establish facts relevant to the obligation of the medium to publish reply. Depending on the court's findings, the complaint may be rejected or accepted. In case of the latter, the defendant will be ordered to publish the reply in due time and the manner. Unsatisfied parties may file an appeal against the court's judgment not later than five days from the date of delivery, and within the same period the Court must decide upon appeal. The attested copy of the final judgment shall be submitted to the media, which is obliged to keep all broadcast recordings for at least thirty days upon their publication and to make them available to persons who have right to reply (Article 33).

234. The right to reply is also determined in the Codex of Montenegrin Journalists in the following manner. Principle IV of the Codex of Montenegrin Journalists, 2016 specifies the duty of a journalist to correct/complete previous incomplete/incorrect information especially the one that can cause any harm and at the same time to make sure that the correction is pointed out in the adequate manner. The Guidelines state that if a media outlet has published a report containing a significant distortion of the facts, it must publish a correction promptly in the same space or within the same program (with due/comparable prominence). Also, when media has published an erroneous report that has caused harm to a person's or institution's reputation, it must publish an apology promptly and with due prominence.

122. As stipulated in the Art. 11, "on the basis of the State Attorney's proposal, the competent court may ban the distribution of the publicized media programming that: invites forceful destruction of the constitutional system and violation of the territorial integrity of the Republic; infringes on the guaranteed human and citizen's freedoms and rights; or instigates national, racial or religious intolerance or hatred."

235 – 238

Chapter 4. Political Broadcasting

235. Freedom of expression during political campaigning has two important dimensions. First, it assumes the right to inform the electoral body by generating their opinion and second, it is a right to freely express their votes. Regarding the first one, every voter has the right to be objectively informed on the candidates, lists, programs, and other relevant issues regarding the upcoming election. The informing process is usually conducted through media presentations and through their presence in political gatherings and other events organized during the campaign period. Since media presentation of the parties is very relevant, these issues along with the financial aspect of it, are treated by law.[123] Second element is expressed via the right to freely and openly vote for the candidate. This element has to be ensured by the state not only to provide the accurate procedure and spatial capacities, but to protect voters from threats and pressures. Electoral law stipulates through the general principle that the voters have the right to be informed about the activities and programs during the electoral campaign.

236. Both dimensions of these rights are implicitly protected under the criminal legislation. The Criminal Code of Montenegro, in Chapter 16, delineates a set of crimes against the electoral rights. In accordance with the wording of the Law, these are: Violation of the right of nomination (Article 184), violation of the voting rights (Article 185), violations of freedom of choice in voting (Article 186), misuse of voting rights (Article 187), compiling inaccurate voters' lists (Article 188), preventing maintenance of voting (Article 189), prevention of monitoring voting (Article 190), violation of the secrecy of voting (Article 191), falsification of voting results (Article 192), destruction of documents on voting (Article 193), and other forms of serious offenses against electoral rights (Article 194).[124]

237. There are several legal acts regulating the political advertising in Montenegro: Electoral Law, Law of Public Services Broadcasting, and the Guidelines on the Montenegrin Press Code adopted by Montenegrin MSB. On the one hand, the Law on Amendments of the Electoral law determines different issues relevant for the role of media in the electoral process. On the other hand, the Law on financing political parties, as well as the Law on amendments of the Law on political parties, does not elaborate on the electoral procedure.[125] On the contrary, they stay silent.

238. A significant number of OSCE recommendations were incorporated in the latest version of the Electoral law of 2014, which was confirmed by the Venice Commission. In fact, the 2014 version of Electoral Law clearly defined the obligations

123. Dedović, V., Vujović, Z., *Izborni Sistem U Crnoj Gori In Izborni I Partijski Sistem U Crnoj Gori: Perspektiva razvoja unutarpartijske demokratije*, p. 130).

124. Criminal Code of Montenegro (OG of MNE, No. 70/03, 13/04, 47/06, 40/08, 25/10, 32/11, 40/13, 56/13). V. Dedović and Z. Vujović, *IZBORNI SISTEM U CRNOJ GORI in IZBORNI I PARTIJSKI SISTEM U CRNOJ GORI: Perspektiva razvoja unutarpartijske demokratije*, p. 130.

125. Law on Amendments of Electoral Law (OG of MNE, Nos. 4/98, 05/98, 17/98, 14/00, 18/00, 09/01, 41/02, 46/02, 45/04, 48/06, 56/06, 46/11, 14/14, 47/14). 2. Law on financing political parties (OG of MNE, Nos. 21/04, 73/10, 40/11, 59/11), Law on financing political subjects and electoral campaigning (OG of MNE, No. 52/14).

of media in the election campaign aiming the principle of equality of all actors in the election campaign. In fact, OSCE/ODIHR recommended that in order to ensure equal treatment of all participants in electoral process "public media should ensure a balance in reporting the news and news programmes."[126]

239. Electoral law includes international standards for conducting fair elections. This standard states that candidates, during the election campaign, shall have the right without special approval to convey posters, photographs, advertisements, pamphlets, videos to the public. Furthermore, international standards provide that all participants should be treated equally in the media during the electoral process. It states that all participants "can express their opinions in the main bodies of the media and that all political actors have the ability to hold meetings, including those on public places and distribute propaganda material." Although the international standards of media presentation are mainly incorporated in the laws and implemented in the practice, according to the international organizations, "latent campaigning" by government officials still exists.[127]

240. Article 9 of the Law of Public Services Broadcasting and Article 55 of the Electoral law provide that presentation of participants in election campaigns through public broadcasting agencies shall be carried out based on the rules passed by a relevant authority of the public broadcasting agency. Submitters of candidate lists through commercial and non-profit broadcasting agencies shall be carried out based on the rules to be adopted by the broadcasting agency with the aim to ensure fair editorial policy and equal presentation of submitters of verified lists of candidates (Article 51 of Rules). The commercial and non-profit broadcasting agencies shall adopt the rules and make them accessible to the public no later than ten days from the day of election calling. The same applies to a public broadcasting agency, so that it shall make them accessible at least ten days from the day of election calling. In that regard, RTM shall produce and broadcast programs, with respecting high standards of professional ethics and quality, which shall during the election campaign, on the basis of separate regulations, provide equal presentation of political parties, coalitions and individuals. For example, under this provision of the Law of Public Services Broadcasting, the Council of the RTM before any election campaign has to adopt the rules. In accordance with the current law they were obliged to adopt and publish the terms and conditions of the representation of political parties, candidates and their respective programs, not later than fifteen days after the elections have been scheduled. The rules adopted for the presidential elections of 2008, written under the OSCE expertise, have served as the model for the rules for all upcoming elections. Since 2008, the rules on public coverage on elections have not undergone big changes.[128] On the contrary, the main differences that occurred are in the number and scheduling of political debates.[129] To ensure the

126. Dedović, V., Vujović, Z., *Izborni Sistem U Crnoj Gori In Izborni I Partijski Sistem U Crnoj Gori: Perspektiva razvoja unutarpartijske demokratije*, p. 130.

127. Dedović, V., Vujović, Z., *Izborni Sistem U Crnoj Gori In Izborni I Partijski Sistem U Crnoj Gori: Perspektiva razvoja unutarpartijske demokratije*, p. 130.

128. IRIS Legal Observations of the European Audiovisual Observatory, IRIS 2009-4:15/23, European Audiovisual Observatory, available at: http://merlin.obs.coe.int/article.php?id=11705).

129. Terms and Conditions for the Presentation of Candidates and their Programs for the parliamentary elections, scheduled for March 29, 2009.

transparency of the elections and to enable every citizen to be timely, accurately and impartially informed on all phases of the electoral procedure, RTM in July of 2016, has passed and published two sets of rules regarding the elections on national and local levels. These are Rules on broadcasting the parliamentary elections scheduled for October 16, 2016 and Rules on broadcasting the local elections scheduled for October 16, 2016.[130]

241. The amendments of 2011 to the Electoral law aims at monitoring media conduct during the electoral process. Article 64b of Electoral Law determined that the Parliament, by a special decision, shall establish a board for monitoring the application of the Election Law for the part related to media. The committee has the jurisdiction to monitor and supervise the fulfillment of media obligations in pre-election campaigns, including but not limited to: considering complaints on actions of the media, deciding on and concluding on such complaints; warning media to act adequately and eliminate potential irregularities; issuing the opinions; publishing its positions on violation of the media standards, in order to undertake measures against the media acting contrary to the Law.

242. The Law specifies that the Board shall consist of ten members and shall be composed on parity on the basis of MPs of the Parliamentary majority and Parliamentary opposition. Chairperson and Deputy Chairperson of the Board shall be appointed from the members of the Board. The Board shall be established no later than ten days from the day of the start of the election campaign for MPs. Proposal for appointment of the Chairperson, Deputy Chairperson, and members of the Board shall be submitted to the Parliament by the working body of the Parliament in charge of election and appointments.

243. The Guidelines of the Montenegrin Press Code 2016 provides that reporting on meetings during election campaigns has to be accurate and must not reflect their own views on the political actors. This approach affirms the right of citizens to accurate information and supports the principle of equal opportunities for all political parties and other participants in the electoral process. The Code further states that journalists must respect the procedure of the pre-election silence, without prejudice to their right and obligation to report on all matters of public interest.

§1. Rules on Political Independence of Broadcasters

244. Political independence of broadcasters is an intrinsic part of a democratic system. Electoral rights are exercised proportionally with the right to be informed by media about the electoral programs and activities of electoral lists, as well as the candidates from the electoral lists.

245. Media outlets are obliged to consistently apply the principle of equality for all actors in the electoral process, as stated in Article 9 of the Electoral Law (EL). The Law specifies the rules on the representation of the candidates, electoral lists, and political parties through the media during the electoral campaign. It is envisaged that the participants of the election are entitled to present themselves through the national

130. Rules on programme schedule for Election of 2016, available at: http://www.RTM.me/RTM/dokumenti/regulativa.html.

public broadcaster—Radio Television of Montenegro and via regional and local public broadcasters. It further states that the actors in the electoral process have the right to inform the citizens about their candidates, programs, lists, and activities in the same day in the same amount of time and free of charge. In addition to the provisions governing the presentation through media, the law also regulates the issues of participation of public officials in the electoral process and certain restrictions on their public appearances in the campaign carries; restrictions on the use of state assets (money, technical resources, space, equipment, public enterprises, public institutions and funds, local government units etc.).[131]

246. The Electoral Law also specifies that from the day of verifying the list of candidates to the completion of the election propaganda, the submitters of lists of candidates shall promote their candidates, programs, and activities, through the national public broadcasting agency Radio–Television of Montenegro, as well as through regional and local public broadcasting agencies, in the same daily timing and/or rubrics, on daily basis, in equal duration and free of charge. Promotion of their programs and announcements of their gatherings can also be organized via shows and/or columns of commercial public media, and commercial advertising space, with payment of relevant consideration and as agreed with the broadcasting agency (Article 50 EL).

§2. Fair Representation in Election Periods

247. In accordance with the OSCE/ODIHR recommendation, public broadcasters shall ensure equal treatment of all participants in the electoral process, including a balance in reporting the news and news programs. The Electoral law provides that the RTM, national, regional, and local public radio-broadcasting agencies shall be obliged to provide presentation of all submitters of verified candidate lists, and their understanding of the electoral process, every day, "in equal duration and at the same time, fully free of charge and equally, within their political newscasts and in precisely defined political marketing blocks, which can be heard and watched in the entire territory of Montenegro and/or local self-governments."

248. As provided in Article 51a, the governing political parties through state officials and local self-government officials may make presentations as representatives of candidate lists in electronic public, commercial and non-profit media outlets. The officials are not allowed to misuse or use their media presentation in the role of the government or other public officials for advertising or indirect advertising of the candidate list and/or their election program. Editors, journalists and hosts of political-informative, cultural, documentary and sports programs on electronic public, commercial and non-profit media are obliged, by means of their professional and impartial behavior, not to allow indirect advertising of election programs of submitters of candidate lists by the officials for the purpose of ensuring equal presentation of all participants to the election process during the election campaign. As stated in the last amendments of Electoral law, media outlet may decide not to air texts or programs that would imply party affiliation or have party propaganda nature when reporting on the current events and work of state authorities and officials.

131. V. Dedović and Z. Vujović, *supra.* , p. 130.

§3. News and Current Affairs Programs

249. RTM has a precisely defined obligation to: "organize and broadcast on weekly basis no less than two hour-and-a-half shows of confrontation of submitters of verified candidate lists and candidates from such lists within political newscast broadcasted between 8pm and 11pm, as agreed between editorial team and submitters of candidate lists." The list of questions to be the topic of the show shall be mutually agreed with submitters. Also, editors and hosts of the shows shall be obliged to treat all participants in confrontation shows impartially and equally (Article 56). All other commercial media outlets are free to organize news and current affair programs under the general rule of the equal representation of the all political subjects during the election campaign.

§4. Political Advertising

250. Political advertising during the election campaign period has its own rules which are often, even in more democratic countries misused.

251. The last amendments to the Electoral law, in Article 53a, provide that Television of Montenegro and Radio of Montenegro during the election campaign period shall be obliged "to provide each submitter of a verified candidate list with free, equal, and daily broadcasting within all commercial marketing blocks and within political newscasts on a TV channel, or within a Radio program which can be watched and heard on the entire territory of Montenegro." This refers to: (1) Political and propaganda TV-clips or audio-clips in all political marketing blocks, the duration of which is not less than 200 seconds a day, depending on the planned number of advertising blocks of political marketing; (2) Three-minute coverage of the promotional gathering, twice a day, at the time immediately after the central evening informative TV and Radio shows. The production of content shall be the obligation of the submitters of lists of candidates being promoted. The law specifies that regional and local public radio-broadcasting agencies shall have the same obligation as the national one. It shall be obliged to provide each submitter of verified candidate list with free, equal, and daily broadcasting space within commercial marketing blocks which can be watched and heard on the entire territory of the local self-government.

252. RTM and broadcasting agencies shall not be allowed, "under any conditions, to enable the presentation and reasoning of election programme of submitters of lists of candidates or their indirect advertising outside the time." Candidates and submitters of candidates list shall pay for marketing content when broadcast via a commercial broadcasting agency (Article 54 of the Electoral Law).

253. Presentation of submitters of candidate lists through commercial and non-profit broadcasting agencies shall be carried out based on the rules to be adopted by the broadcasting agency with the aim to ensure fair editorial policy and equal presentation of submitters of verified lists of candidates. The commercial and non-profit broadcasting agencies shall adopt the rules and make them accessible to the public no later than ten days from the day of election calling (Article 51 EL).

254. Within the general principles of the Codex of Montenegrin Journalists, 2015 under its Guidelines, there is the rule on the Rallies during Election Campaign. When contributing from rallies organized during an election campaign, the reporters will also report on the views and values with which they may not agree. Such an approach is a matter of reporter's fairness; it serves the citizens' right to the freedom of information and supports the principle of equal opportunities for all political parties and other participants in the election process.

Chapter 5. Advertising Rules

255. Audiovisual commercial service in Montenegro is based on the principle of freedom of advertising and sponsorship, and recognizability of advertisers and sponsors. There are certain obligations that have to be fulfilled so that advertisements shall be accurate, complete, and specific. Advertiser, ordering party, or sponsor shall not have any editorial influence on the program content, scheduling of the sponsored services or programs, or the responsibility or editorial independence of a broadcaster. The ordering party shall be responsible for the accuracy of advertisements, while the broadcaster shall be responsible for their compliance with the provisions of the Electronic Media Law, the Media Law, and this Rulebook (Articles 11–12 of the RACC). Advertising activity of the ACC, as provided under the Article 8 of LEM, is a service which also assumes the program on direct or indirect promotion of goods, services, or the image of a natural or legal entity pursuing an economic activity, in return for payment or for similar consideration. Standards, conditions, and quotas for advertising, teleshopping, and sponsorship in the electronic media programs (the radio and television programs) and electronic publications are in details regulated in accordance with several bylaws, defined under the Rulebook on ACC. However, along with the Rulebook there are separate several documents regulating the advertising of individual products or services—prohibiting or limiting the advertising in certain media. These rules are fully harmonized with the regulations of the EU. In accordance with Media Law, Law on Electronic Media, and other international standards of good business practice and professional ethics, advertising, teleshopping, and sponsorship are free, providing the same rights and obligations of domestic and foreign legal and natural persons.

256. For the last several years, the advertising rules have been the subject of several NGOs reports and analysis of the advertising market in Montenegro, emphasizing that state money for advertising has not been distributed adequately. Furthermore, they have stated that the financing of the media and its ownership have to be more transparent, and visible. Since Montenegrin market is small, and the number of the media outlet is high, their activities are often not profitable, so that this problem is even more apparent. According to available data gathered via questionnaires distributed to the media and governments institutions, the CCE Report stated that the total media advertising market in Montenegro in 2014 was worth around EUR 9 million. Out of this sum, at least 2.12 million came from the state budget. These figures are not official, but convey the results of a recently conducted research by an NGO project. They state that almost 50% of the institutions and companies did not respond to the questionnaire. However, they provided the public with an estimation that the Public Broadcasting Service has received EUR 150,000 in 2014 and Pobjeda, daily paper, EUR 130,000 (9% of the total). On the other hand, Dan, the daily with the most widespread distribution manages to earn only 2% of the money that is set aside for advertising. On the basis of this estimation, the several Montenegrin NGOs stated that this statistics have proven the practice of "selective financing which ensures the influence on the media and threatens competition."[132]

257. However, this problem seems to have been overstated. Article 16 of the Law on Prevention of Illegal Business specifies that all media outlets in Montenegro are obliged to, before the publication of advertisements and commercials, obtain certain information from the clients. It also stipulates the duty of the media to keep records on data of clients (name, residence, address, identification or registration number) and quarterly inform the tax authority of all these details. Full adherence to the implementation of the text shall provide for transparency, and thereby elimination of previously described practice.

§1. Various Forms of Commercial Communication

258. There are different types of ACCs introduced in the Law on Electronic Media, and in the Rulebook on Audiovisual Commercial Communications ("RACC"), such as: Advertising (Comparative advertising, Deceptive advertising, Surreptitious advertising, Teleshopping, Split-screen advertising, Virtual Advertising, Telepromotion and radiopromotion), Sponsorship, and Product Placement (Article 88 of LEC).

259. As provided under the Article 4 of RACC, advertising may involve any form of announcement broadcast whether in return for payment or for similar consideration or broadcast for self-promotional purposes by any legal or natural person in order to present or draw attention to a certain product or service, including immovable property, rights and obligations, or to encourage the consumers to use or buy that product or service, in return for payment. Comparative advertising is directly or indirectly related to a competitor, deceptive advertising misleads or is likely to mislead the target audience affecting their economic behavior, whereas surreptitious advertising is present through "the activities of a producer of goods or a provider of services in radio and/or television programmes when such representation is intended by the media service provider to serve as advertising and might mislead the public as to its nature." The LEM further states that teleshopping involves the direct offering of goods, services, and immovable property, in return for payment, split-screen advertising of the editorial contents simultaneously or in parallel while virtual advertising is conveyed via inserting of a new advertisement in such a way that it appears to be an integral part of the original transmission of the program. Telepromotion and radiopromotion are "advertising based on the interruption of programs, during which presenters take over the role of promoters

132. CCE, Equal chances with all media outlets in Montenegro, CGO, 2015, available at: http://media.cgo-cce.org/2014/12/cgo-cce-jednake-sanse-za-sve-medije-u-CG-2014.pdf, CCE, How much and to whom do the citizens of Montenegro pay for advertising?, 2012 available at: http://media.cgo-cce.org/2015/12/cgo-cce-how-much-and-to-whom-do-the-citizens-in-mne-pay-for-adv.pdf, CCE, How much, to which media and related agencies did municipalities in Montenegro pay for their services, 2012 available at: http://media.cgo-cce.org/2015/12/cgo-cce-how-much-to-which-media-and-related-agencies-did-municipalities-in-mne-pay-for-their-services.pdf, CCE, How much, to which media and related agencies did municipalities in Montenegro pay for their services, 2013 available at: http://media.cgo-cce.org/2015/12/cgo-cce-how-much-and-to-whom-do-the-citizens-in-mne-pay-for-adv-2012.pdf.

of certain goods or services." Sponsorship implies "any contribution made by a natural or a legal entity not engaged in providing AVM services or in the production of audiovisual works, to the financing of radio and/or television programs with a view to promoting its name, its trademark, its image, its attractiveness, its products or services." Product placement as an ACC "consists of indication within the program of a product, a service or the trademark thereof, in return for payment or for similar consideration."

§2. Restrictions on Content

260. All legislative pieces such as the Media law, the Law on Electronic Media, and the Rulebook on the Programme Standards in Electronic Media have a clear and precise set of rules forbidding or limiting the specific advertising content. For example, the Media law, in Article 24 stipulates grounds for forbidding certain contents, so that advertising of the certain programs products or activities (such as transaction of the human organs or tissues for transfusion, the weapons, narcotics, tobacco products, traffic of commodities etc.) is prohibited (Article 24 ML).

261. Article 22 of ML, specifies that any program that could endanger any aspect of a child's well-being shall be previously marked in an obvious way. The identity of the minor involved in a criminal act, either in the capacity of a victim or a defendant. As an exception to it, the identity of a minor, sentenced for a criminal offense by a final judgment, may be published if there is an overriding interest of the public to be informed. Further, LEM Article 48(3) specifies that "publication of information revealing the identity of a minor less than 18 years of age involved in any case of violence, regardless of whether being a witness, a victim or an offender, or disclosing any particulars of the family relations and private life of a child is prohibited." Portraying minors in situations that are vulgar, violent, and detrimental to their mental and physical development and life (including the scenes showing minors use alcohol, tobacco, or other harmful substances) are also prohibited. Minors are strongly protected under the RPSEM (Articles 19–28). The ACC shall not include the content that could cause damage to minors, by causing fear of aggressiveness or inadequate and unacceptable moral and social conduct. The Rules provide that the ACC shall not promote alcoholic beverages or products nor encourage minors to purchase or persuade their parents or others to purchase the advertised goods. Furthermore, when there are certain features of the program that involve minors, minors cannot be presented in a sexual way nor represent men and women as boys or girls with sexual features of the adults; they cannot be shown in dangerous situations, such as: climbing unprotected areas; entering unknown facilities; talking to strange people; using lighters, petrol, medicines and electrical household appliances, or in other situations jeopardizing their health and lives. Abusing the confidence minors place in other people, undermining the reputation or authority of parents, siblings or other family members, pedagogues, teachers shall also be prohibited. Broadcasted contents shall pay attention to promotion of the healthy lifestyle and balanced eating. In that regard, promotion of breast milk substitutes is prohibited. Under Article 27 of the Rulebook, ACC related to toys and educational products for minors shall not be misleading as to: nature, function, and size of a toy;

level of ability/skill necessary to operate a toy; description of accessories included or not included in the toy packaging; toy's price and if additional products are needed in order to use it; minimizing the price of products or suggesting that it can be afforded by the budget of every family.

262. With regard to protection against discrimination, the Law on Electronic Media (LEM) and Media Law similarly addresses this issue so that Article 48(2) of LEM states that an AVM service shall not directly or indirectly: instigate any kind of discrimination, especially on the grounds of race, skin color, sex, national or social origin, birth, religion, political or other belief, sexual or other orientation, property status, culture, language, age, mental or physical disability, or promote social discrimination on the grounds of physical appearance or success based on the weight loss or other aesthetic categories. Article 23 of ML provides that it is forbidden to publish information and opinions that instigate discrimination, hatred or violence against persons or group of persons based on their belonging or not-belonging to a certain religion, ethnic group, race, nation, sex or sexual orientation.

263. The RACC is extensive in prohibiting specific content. They go further and prohibit: "prejudice respect for human dignity; encourage behavior prejudicial to people's health or safety; trade in human organs or tissue for transplantation or transfusion; escort agencies; pornography; unscientific contents and methods for health problems, creates or maintains monopoly bookmaking, games of chance and gambling, surreptitious and deceptive, vague or ambiguous expressions, or misleading data, encourage behavior prejudicial to the protection of the environment; include the scenes of death, injuries, violence of devastation of property and nature; promote tobacco and tobacco products, narcotics and psychoactive substances, weapon, ammunition and pyrotechnical devices and the trade in goods and services prohibited by law; promote medicinal products available only on prescription and medical treatment that is not in compliance with a separate law regulating healthcare; use visual and audio forms, contents or elements recognizable as news or announcements (bulletin, news, etc.); use recognizability of certain program with an intention to mislead viewers; discredit or denigrate a competitor, and its products or services; copy the advertising content, activities, products or services of another advertiser; use the trademark or other recognizable feature of a competitor, without authorization; send messages using the techniques affecting sub-consciousness, which are manipulative or harmful in either social or emotional sense; promote paranormal phenomena and parapsychology (Article 7).

264. The RACC, Article 13 establishes the aim of avoiding deceptive programs related to: "features of goods or services, such as the type, composition, manner and date of production, manner and time of provision of service, availability, quantity, specification, manner of use, suitability for certain purposes, geographic or commercial origin, results that can be expected from the use of goods or services, results and other material indicators of tests or control of the goods or services; price or manner of calculation of price, as well as the conditions of sale of goods or provision of service; nature, features and rights of advertisers, such as their identity, property, qualifications, industrial, commercial or intellectual property, awards, recognitions they received." The advertisements shall not describe any offer as "free" if there are certain expenses (all charges, taxes, levies) for the consumer.

265. Under Article 15 of RACC, comparative advertising shall be permitted if: it compares goods or services meeting the same needs; it is not deceptive and it objectively compares one or more material; it does not create confusion among traders, the advertiser and a competitor; it does not discredit or denigrate the goods, services, trademarks, trade names, other distinguishing marks, activities, or circumstances of a competitor; for products with designation of origin, it relates to products with the same designation; it does not take unfair advantage of the reputation of a trademark, trade name or other distinguishing marks of a competitor; it does not take unfair advantage of the designation of origin of competing products or services; it does not generate abuse of confidence, dependence, lack of experience or knowledge, and superstition; it does not contain encouragement of violence or unjustified fear (Articles 16-17). ACC abusing people's care for their health or environment shall be prohibited. ACC shall not include inaccurate or misleading claims by highlighting the expressions such as "environmentally safe," "not harmful for the environment," "eco-food," "health food" and similar words or symbols with the same meaning (Article 18).

266. Media law, in Article 24, stipulates grounds for forbidding certain contents, so that advertising transaction of the human organs or tissues for transfusion, medicines and medical treatments available only with the medical prescription, curing procedures and methods is prohibited (Article 24 ML). In the same manner, Rules provide that ACC shall not promote medicines, and medicinal material available only on prescription, or the medicinal procedures, healthcare methods, or treatments that are not in compliance with separate laws regulating healthcare. Healthcare institutions shall be allowed to advertise only: the name of healthcare institution, its activity, address and telephone number, and its working hours (Articles 29 and 30 of RACC). Advertisements of medicinal products available without prescription shall contain the information on the name, indications, and warnings. Advertisements may include only the information in line with the approved overview of the main features of a medicine, which is included in a license for sale of this medicine, issued by the public administration authority in charge of medicines and medicinal products (Article 31). Advertisement of medicinal products shall not claim that effects of the products or service are guaranteed and shall include an instruction that the medicinal product can be used only with medical consultation, unless it is available without prescription (Article 32).

267. Advertising and teleshopping promoting of some products can be conducted only under certain conditions. For example: the advertising of the alcoholic beverages shall not suggest or create an impression that consumption of alcoholic beverages could improve a physical condition or driving skills, or contribute to social or sexual success or solution of personal conflicts; or improve therapeutic features (Article 34 of RACC). In the same manner, in accordance with the prohibition stated in Article 24 of ML, RACC provide that ACC shall not promote tobacco and tobacco products. The advertisements shall not: depict smoking or imitation of smoking, tobacco products, their packaging, or tobacco smoke, and use a trademark or other sign of the producers of tobacco products. On the other hand, the prohibitions of the promotion of tobacco does not apply to the advertisements recommending quitting, breaking the habit of smoking or campaigning against smoking.

§3. Time and Frequency Restrictions

268. The general terms on transmission time are defined under Article 59 of the LEM. In fact, it states that day transmission time includes all programs within a radio or television broadcast from zero to twenty-four hours, in the calendar year (January 1 and December 31). At least twelve hours of programs is the obligation of broadcaster on daily basis. At least 10% of total weekly air time has to be assigned to news and current affairs: thirty minutes of news a day within which it should have at television program (Article 59).

269. Also, the duration of advertising and teleshopping shall be calculated for the period between zero and twenty-four hours. Teleshopping windows shall be of a minimum uninterrupted duration of fifteen minutes. However, under Article 90 of LEM states that: free of charge announcements of public works and humanitarian events; free of charge presentation of works of art and publication of data on producers, organizers, sponsors or donors of works of art, culture and art events and charity events; and information about and promotion of own programs, shall not be deemed as advertising. Form and scheduling of advertising and teleshopping is also defined under the Articles 37–55 of RACC in the same manner as in the bylaw. It further states that advertising and teleshopping shall be readily recognizable and distinguishable from other contents by acoustic, optical and/or spatial means. They shall be broadcast in blocks.

270. The advertisements of public authorities and organizations, local authorities, and public services shall not use the name, image, or personal feature of a public official, or an official of a public authority, organization, of local authority. The advertisements shall be used, directly or indirectly, to advertise a political organization or some other organization established by a public authority, political party or a politician. The proportion of advertising spots in programs of public broadcasters within a given clock hour shall not exceed 10% (six minutes), whereas together with teleshopping spots, per hour during a day, it shall not exceed 15% (nine minutes) (Article 92). In the commercial broadcasters it goes up to the 15% (nine minutes), while that proportion of advertising and teleshopping spots, within a given clock hour during the day, shall not exceed 20% (twelve minutes) (Article 93 LEM).

271. As a general rule, advertisements might be broadcast between the programs "if it does not violate the continuity and value of the programme or infringes copyrights." Advertisements shall not be broadcast during some type of program such as: religious services, formal ceremonies, live coverage of Parliament sessions, programs on major tragic events etc. If a program contains separate parts or if a covered event has breaks, it can be inserted between the parts of the program. If news programs last longer than thirty minutes on TV channels, and longer than ten minutes on radio stations, advertisements may be broadcast only between their parts (political news, sports news, weather) not more than once for no longer than sixty seconds (Articles 42-44 of RACC).

272. As stated on several occasions already, the Agency of Electronic Media has conducted monitoring with the aim to determine the implementation of the regulation on program standards stipulated in the Law on Electronic Media, and Rules on program standards in electronic media outlets. The Agency has monitored the program standards for a period of seven days, from November 5 to 11, from 6 p.m. to 12 p.m. The monitoring has been conducted on the programs of the one public broadcaster TVCG1, and four private commercial broadcasters such as TV Vijesti, TV Prva, TV PINK, and TV Atlas.[133]

273. Also, the standard set in Articles 40(1) and 41(2) of the RACC regarding advertising and teleshopping, specifies that this content shall not exceed 15% (nine minutes) within a given clock hour in the programs of public broadcasters. It also further states that the same type of programs (advertising and teleshopping) in the commercial broadcasters shall not exceed 20% (twenty minutes) within a given clock hour. Regarding this criteria, the Agency, in seven days period, has found nineteen violations of this standard in the following manner: TV PINK—14, TV Atlas—3, TV Prva—2, whereas TVCG and TV Vijesti have not violated this rule. With respect to the standard of the advertising during the news program, the RACC in Article 33 specifies that if news programs such as TV Journals, news bulletins, last longer than thirty minutes when broadcast on TV channels, and longer than ten minutes when broadcast on radio stations, advertisements may be broadcast only between their parts (political news, sports news, weather) not more than once for no longer than sixty seconds. Regarding this rule, the analysis of the Agency in its report stated that none of the TV channels have violated this standard.

274. With respect to the live coverage of programs, the advertisements shall be allowed during the so-called natural breaks (Article 47). RACC specifies that during live TV coverage of sporting events, the advertisements can be inserted during intermissions (e.g., half time, between races, etc.). It further states that "in live coverage of the events longer than sixty minutes, breaks may be taken at points such as half times, or where the focus of coverage shifts from one point to another of the event (e.g., after a resume of the current placing in a race and before refocusing on a particular section of the race)." Breaks may be taken where the commentator finishes discussing one item in the program and moves to another (Article 48 of RACC).

275. Under Article 49, in the case of cultural and art programs, advertisements may inserted if: "there is a clearly marked and dramatically significant lapse of time in the action; there is a complete change of scene, with a significant break in the continuity of action; in the original intervals in the stage play." A break in the documentary and discussion programs may be taken when: there is a change of topic; new participants are introduced.

276. Advertisements during broadcasting of films made for television, excluding series and documentaries, may be inserted once for each period of thirty minutes. The same applies for the children's programs, if duration of the program is longer than thirty minutes (Article 50 of the RACC).

277. When it comes to the transmission of the musical programs, the Article 51 of RACC stated that it may be interrupted at the end of a musical composition or between the acts of an opera or a ballet.

133. Agency of Electronic Media, Report on the Application of the Programme Standards in Audio-Visual Communications in Electronic Media, January 2016, available at: http://www.ardcg.org/index.php?option=com_docman&task=cat_view&gid=43&Itemid=26.

§4. Sponsorship

278. Sponsorship as a type of ACC is defined under the Law on Electronic Media, as the programs which shall meet the following requirements stated under the Article 95 of LEM. These requirements are: (1) the sponsor shall not determine the contents sponsored or the responsibility or editorial independence of the AVM service provider; (2) the program shall not directly encourage the purchase or rental of goods or services, in particular by making special promotional references to those goods or services; (3) sponsored services and programs shall be clearly identified as such; (4) sponsored programs shall be clearly identified by the name, logo and/or other symbol of the sponsor such as a reference to its product(s) or service(s) or a distinctive sign thereof in an appropriate way for programs at the beginning, during and/or at the end of the programs; (5) the sponsor "shall not be legal or natural persons whose principal activity is the manufacture or sale of products or provision of services whose advertising is prohibited by law or whose activities include the manufacture or sale of medicinal products, procedures, and products available only on prescription or prohibited by law;" (6) some kind of programs such as sport, culture, and art allow the sponsor identification only at the beginning and the end of natural breaks. This Article prohibits certain type of sponsors and some type of programs to be sponsored such as: news and current affairs programs, children's programs, and religious programs. Political parties, and other political organizations may not sponsor programs.

279. The modus of operandi and content of the cooperation between the electronic media outlet and the sponsor shall be legally defined. According to the Article 57 of Rulebook, a sponsor and an electronic media outlet shall conclude a program sponsorship agreement, with the specified rights and obligations. At the request of the Agency, the electronic media are obliged to submit the program sponsorship agreements they have concluded. The Agency is obliged to take the confidentiality matters into consideration and protect the documents—contracts, if they are of a confidential nature. The Rules confirm the condition set by the law regarding: identification of the program, referral to type of program, recognizability of the program etc. As specified under Article 59 sponsorship is not advertising and it shall not be included in the total duration of advertising. Sponsorship of news and current affairs programs shall be prohibited. Also, all previously mentioned prohibitions regarding the content and the sponsors' positions (Political parties, coalitions, and other political organizations) are by the RACC determined in the same manner. Thus, the RACC elaborate that: the programs for minors and programs dedicated to automobiles or drivers shall not be sponsored by producers of alcoholic beverages; sponsors' logos shall not be displayed during the children's documentary and religious programs; and a sponsor shall not violate the integrity of the sponsored arts, sports or, cultural programs of its sponsorship. Imitation of another sponsor or its products and activity is strictly prohibited by RACC. (Article 64). Under Article 67 of RACC, the broadcast media are obliged to provide proportional representation of interests of each sponsor in accordance to their share and to inform potential sponsors about the identity of the current sponsors.

280. The Law provides for the right of the Agency or any person whose right or interest has been jeopardized or damaged by advertising to request from the media access to an advertisement broadcast (Article 71). During a period of thirty days from its broadcasting, media outlet is obliged to keep the recording of every advertisement.

§5. Product Placement

281. Generally speaking, product placement is prohibited in Montenegro. This concept in broadcasting law is defined in the Law of Electronic Media which strictly provides for the two group situations in which product placement is allowed: (1) in cinematographic works, films and series, sports and entertainment programs, except children's programs; and (2) where there is no payment but certain goods or services—solely of goods or services of substantial value, are included in the program—free of charge. The Council of Agency of Electronic Media[134] has the competence on deciding the manner for determining the substantial value of goods or services. Montenegrin law, under Article 96 of LEM provides on the legal requirements which have to be fulfilled in order to have programs with the product placement: *First*, the content, and the scheduling shall in no circumstances be influenced in such a way as to affect the responsibility and editorial independence of the AVM provider; *Second,* the content shall not directly encourage the purchase or rental of goods or services, in particular by making special promotional references to those goods or services or by giving prominence to the product; *Third,* in the beginning and at the end of the program and after an advertising break, in order to avoid any confusion, the audience shall be clearly informed of the existence of product placement by appropriate identification.

134. Agency for Electronic Media is an independent AVM service regulatory body founded by the state. It is an autonomous legal entity, acting in public interest.

Chapter 6. Right to Information

§1. Access to Major Events

282. Right to information, as repeated a numerous times throughout the text,[135] has been widely recognized in the several Montenegrin legislative pieces: The Law on Free Access to Information, The Electoral Law, Media Law, and Decision on the List of the Events of Major Importance for the Public in Montenegro.

283. LEM states that a television broadcaster under the jurisdiction of Montenegro shall not exercise their exclusive rights in such a way that a substantial proportion of the public in an EU Member State or the state party to the international treaty binding Montenegro is deprived of the possibility of following events of major importance for society and which are in line with its domestic legislation designated for whole or partial live coverage, or where necessary or appropriate for objective reasons in the public interest, whole or partial deferred coverage on free television (Article 66). Furthermore, this Article provides that a broadcaster may not be granted the right to broadcast on exclusive basis events of major importance for Montenegrin public "unless they are able to ensure following of such events by live coverage or deferred coverage on free television for at least 60% of Montenegro's population or if additional payment would be needed for following such broadcasts." The right to broadcast on an exclusive basis an event of major importance will be granted to several broadcasters if they ensure good quality reception of television program for at least 85% of Montenegro's population.

284. Drawing up a list of national or non-national events of major importance for Montenegro's society is in the hands of the Council. Law stipulates that Council shall determine whether these events should be available by whole or partial live coverage, or where necessary or appropriate for objective reasons in the public interest, whole or partial deferred coverage. Such decision and a list shall be sent to the European Commission, the Standing Committee for Transfrontier Television and state parties to the European Convention on Transfrontier Televisions and international treaties binding Montenegro (Article 67).

285. In accordance with the Law on Electronic Media, the Statute of the AEM, the Law on Ratification of the European Convention on Transfrontier Television, the Decision on the list of events of Major Importance for the Public in Montenegro (Decision) provides and prescribes the events of major importance for the public in Montenegro. It determines whether the event shall be available for whole or partial live coverage or where necessary or appropriate for objective reasons in the public interest, whole or partial deferred coverage. The Decision[136] prescribes the following events as those of major importance for the public in Montenegro: Inauguration of the President of Montenegro; Extraordinary Parliament sessions; Summer and Winter

135. Right to information has been covered in paras: 30, 73, 101, 119.

136. Decision on the List of Events of Major Importance for the Public in Montenegro (OG of MNE, No. 11/12).

Olympic Games; World and European Football Championship, semi-final and final matches, as well as all matches featuring the national team of Montenegro, as well as the opening matches of these championships; Football competitions "Champions League" and "European Cup," semi-final and final matches, as well as all matches featuring the national team of Montenegro, as well as the opening matches of these competitions; All matches of the national team of Montenegro (senior men), both at home and away; Final match of the Football Cup of Montenegro; Tennis tournaments ("Australian open," "Wimbledon," "French Open," "United States Open," "Roland Garros") if Montenegrin representatives participate; Finals and semi-finals of the World and European Basketball Championships if the national team of Montenegro (senior) participates; Finals and semi-finals of the World and European Handball Championships if the national team of Montenegro (senior) participates; Finals and semi-finals of the World and European Volleyball Championships if the national team of Montenegro (senior) participates; Finals and semi-finals of the Handball Champions League if Montenegrin teams participate; Finals and semi-finals of the World and European Water Polo Championships if the national team of Montenegro (senior) participates.

286. When deciding on whether the whole live coverage shall be provided, Article 3 of this Decision provides for one main criteria: if the event is of major importance for the public in Montenegro. The events of major importance for the public in Montenegro shall be provided via whole or partial deferred coverage. The Decision also provides rules in case there are two or more events at the same time. If two or more events take place at the same time, direct coverage of only one of them is justified. If an event takes place with considerable time difference, whether deferred coverage would enable a larger part of the population of Montenegro to view that event.

§2. Short News Reporting

287. Under Article 69 of the LEM, a piece of news lasting not more than ninety seconds published within news programs is deemed to be short information. The right to short information shall be exercised in a way that does not interrupt the course of the event. "When an event of high interest for the public consists of several organizationally independent events, in light of exercising the right to short information, each independent event is deemed an event of special interest for the public. When an event of high interest for the public lasts more than two days, the broadcaster has the right each day to produce short information of the event." Furthermore, Article 69 states that the broadcaster who exercised the right to short information "must enable non-recurrent use of the event footage to another broadcaster unable to shoot the event and has the right to seek compensation of the proportional share of actually incurred costs, and featuring its name in the announcement. The right to short information may be established even in regards to access to major events for the society not broadcasted as per exclusive rights" (Article 69).

288. For the purpose of short news reports, any broadcaster established in the EU or a state party to an international treaty binding Montenegro, has access under equal terms to events of high interest to the public which are transmitted on an exclusive basis by broadcasters under the jurisdiction of Montenegro. "If another broadcaster established in Montenegro as the broadcaster seeking access has acquired exclusive rights to the event of high interest to the public, access shall be sought from that broadcaster. The Council of public broadcaster shall set more detailed conditions for acquiring the right of access to these events by allowing broadcasters to freely choose short extracts from the transmitting broadcaster's signal. A broadcaster may acquire access to these events or use footage of another broadcaster with exclusive rights to the broadcasted event of high interest for the public. Short extracts shall be used solely for general news programs, and may be used in on-demand AVM services only if the same program is offered on a deferred basis by the same AVM service provider" (Article 68).

Chapter 7. Access to Networks

289. According to Montenegrin law, as provided in the Article 37 of the LEC, electronic communications network is presented on the Montenegrin market through the variety of elements of transmission systems, switching, and routing devices, passive network elements enabling the conveyance of signals (by wire, radio, optical or other electromagnetic systems), electric power cable systems used for signal transmission, networks used for broadcasting and distribution of media content to the end users etc. An electronic communications network is considered public when it enables transmission between network termination points and used for electronic communications services. Whereas "electronic communications service" is defined as the transfer of signals via electronic communications networks, including telecommunications services and the service of broadcasting of media content, it does not include media content service provision or editorial control over media.

§1. Must-Carry Rules

290. Must-carry rules in Montenegro have been recently determined by several legal texts such as: Law on Electronic Communications, the Digital Broadcasting Law (DBL), the Law on Electronic Media, Digital Switchover Strategy, 2008 and Agency's plan for Allocation of Radio Frequencies for Digital Terrestrial Broadcasting (determining the technical requirements and the method of using individual radio frequencies and geographic areas).

291. The Law on electronic communications defines the elements of electronic communications network and infrastructure as well as its facilities, which include fixed or wireless connections, the local loop, access to the physical infrastructure, software systems, information systems and databases for service ordering, maintaining, calculation and billing, fixed and mobile networks, virtual network services.

292. All these provisions define the "network operator" as any legal or physical person with the approval to use frequencies and to broadcast programs through digital terrestrial broadcasting network, whereas the "multiplex operator" is any entity providing public electronic communication services of multiplex management, after obtaining approval (Article 5 Digital Broadcasting Law (DBL)). The ratio between these two entities can be seen through the legal determination that the network operator shall deliver at least one contract concluded with a multiplex operator within a certain time, and that a multiplex operator may also be a network operator. Even if a network operator is at the same time a multiplex operator, the law requests separate accounting. With the aim of more rational use of multiplex capacities, Article 7 of DBL addresses the possibility to divide for provision of audiovisual media services and electronic communication services. Prior to access of allocated multiplex capacity, radio and television programs must be encoded in accordance with the specific encoding standard (ITU-T H.264/AVC), as defined under Article 8 DBL. For the purpose of digital broadcasting of signals of the national broadcasting services, RTM was awarded the right to access the first network multiplex with coverage of the entire territory of

Montenegro, without conducting public call procedure, for transmission of two television programs in the standard quality (SDTV). Access to network multiplex with local coverage shall be awarded without conducting a public call procedure, for the purpose of digitally broadcasting signals from local public broadcasting services in the territory of local government units.

293. The transmission and broadcasting of programs of the national public broadcasting services are in the hands of the Broadcasting Centre founded by the Government of Montenegro. The right to multiplex access for the first network with coverage for the entire territory of Montenegro for providers of audiovisual media services, as well as for other networks, shall be realized through a public call with defined conditions for using capacities for audiovisual media service providers during the switchover period, in order to create conditions for introduction of high definition television (HDTV).

294. DBL provides, in Article 10, two conditions for the digital broadcasting of signals of the national public broadcasting services—RTM: First, development of the first network will be carried out for coverage of the entire territory of Montenegro, that is at least for 85% of the population of Montenegro and second, funds will be provided for coverage of increased costs for electricity in the switchover period for the first network operator (the Budget of Montenegro and donations and loans of European Commission).

§2. Other Access Obligations for Network

295. Under Montenegrin law, the operator shall have the right to negotiate on access to and interconnection of networks "for the purpose of providing publicly available electronic communications services and ensuring their interoperability." The mutual relation—rights and obligations, between the operators shall be determined in the contract signed between the operators by providing the precise information: on the services, agreed quality and time limits, commercial terms, maintenance of network operability, service interoperability, term of the contract, if the contract has been concluded for the indefinite term, procedures for data protection in the course of service provision, sanctions in the event of breach of the contract (Article 56 of Law on Electronic Communications (LEC)). If the operator refuses another operator to access and/or interconnect, the Agency of Electronic Communications shall, upon request, decide on the disputed issues. The Agency may instruct the operators to ensure the appropriate access and/or interconnection for the purpose of ensuring interoperability of electronic communications networks and services. LEC defines that conditional access systems for digital television and radio services must have technical conditions enabling operators to have complete control over services protected with such systems. The operator of conditional access services is obliged to offer all broadcasters whose programs it transmits, the technical conditions, under fair, transparent, and non-discriminatory terms, which allows the end users to access the programs by means of conditional access devices. Conditional access systems used by operators shall not prevent the access to free programs (Article 60).

296. The Agency shall request the specific measures when it considers that "the denial of access would hinder establishment of a sufficiently competitive market at the retail level, or if it would cause harm to the interests of end users." As determined under the Decision on identification of operator with significant market power, the access to, and use of, specific electronic communications network elements, *inter alia,* assumes the following activities: to negotiate in good faith with operators over the different issues in order to enable access to the network; to carry out interconnection of the electronic communications network; to grant free access to different protocols and other technologies indispensable for the interoperability of services and/or networks; to provide adequate technical conditions for the electronic communication infrastructure; to provide facilities necessary for interoperability of services for different types of services (i.e., intelligent networks services). When assessing the scope of obligations in accession process, Agency shall evaluate: "the technical and economic viability of using or installing facilities of a competitor, taking into account the rate of market development and type of the access and/or interconnection; the feasibility of such access; the initial investment of the facility owner; the need to safeguard competition in the long term, particularly economically effective competition at the level of infrastructure; adequate intellectual property rights; provision of services deriving from international obligations of Montenegro." The Agency has the mandate to define the "organizational requirements to be met by the operator with significant market power as well as by the operators requesting access, when this is considered to be a prerequisite for securing the unhindered functioning of the network" (Article 75). While deciding upon the access issues, the Agency might request price controlling of certain services, based on the market analysis. If the Agency finds that the application of regulatory measures did not result in effective market competition due to the important and permanent barriers to the market competition, with the prior Government opinion, Agency may decide to impose the obligation on the vertically integrated operators the obligation to separate their activities. Also, vertically integrated operator with a significant market power on one or more relevant markets may independently decide to separate or transfer its access network (Articles 79–80).

297. The Council of the Agency of Electronic Media can allow simultaneous broadcasting of two or more radio or television programs, lasting up to three hours a day continuously or cumulatively. This is possible only: (1) if this broadcasting does not interfere with the AVM service provision by other broadcasters; and (2) if it does not violate provisions on media concentration rules. The Council may approve the broadcasters' linkage into regional or national networks under certain conditions, as specified under the Article 122 of LEM. Basically, two conditions have to be met: first, the Council needs to approve the joint program (amounting to 10% of own joint programs transmitted over the network a day) of networked broadcasters and has to accept the editor in chief appointing decision fifteen days before the start of broadcasting the joint program; and second, any of the networked broadcasters has to broadcast within the area he has been licensed for, for at least one hour of own production a day between seven and twenty-two hours.

298. Under Article 5 of LEM, Montenegro shall ensure freedom of reception and retransmission of AVM services from EU Member States and other European signatory countries to the European Convention on Transfrontier Television; in certain cases, it may restrict the freedom of reception and retransmission in accordance with international national legal obligations. Under Article 60 of LEM, European audiovisual work means: works originating in EU Member States, works originating in the state parties to the European Convention on Transfrontier Television and works co-produced within the framework of agreements related to the audiovisual sector concluded between EU Member States and third countries. In some cases, as stated in the Article 60, audiovisual works are conditioned so that they shall be: made by one or more producers established in one or more of those States and controlled by one or more producers established in one or more of those States. In addition to it, the same Article specifies that the contribution of co-producers of those States to the total co-production costs is preponderant and the co-production is not controlled by one or more producers established outside those States. Works that are not European but that are produced within the framework of bilateral co-production treaties concluded between EU Member States and third countries shall be deemed to be European works provided that the co-producers from the Community supply a majority share of the total cost of production and that the production is not controlled by one or more producers established outside the territory of the EU Member States. In accordance with the Audiovisual Media Services Directive,[137] a Montenegrin broadcaster shall ensure a share of 51% to European works in its annual transmission time. This percentage does not include time for news, sport events, advertising, teletext, and teleshopping. If a broadcaster has initial share of at least 5% of this work, it will be obliged to increase this percentage as compared to the previous year, under conditions set out by the Agency Council (Article 61).

137. Directive 2010/13/EU of the European Parliament and of the Council of March 10, 2010 on the coordination of certain provisions laid down by law, regulation or administrative action in Member States concerning the provision of audiovisual media services (Audiovisual Media Services Directive).

Chapter 8. Standards and Interoperability

299. The whole concept and functioning of electronic communication networks and electronic communications infrastructure is defined under certain standards. As specified in Article 3 of the Law on Electronic Communications (LEC) these principles are: objectivity; proportionality; transparency; non-discrimination; equal chances and conditions; predictability of business environment; harmonizing electronic communications activities with international standards; ensuring the availability of services to all Montenegrin citizens; ensuring benefits for vulnerable category of persons – persons with reduced mobility or with disabilities; interconnecting electronic communications networks and services; protecting, and promoting competitiveness on the electronic communications market; ensuring protection of users in their relations with operators by enabling efficient dispute resolution procedure; encouraging investments and innovations and improved infrastructure; continuously improving service quality in the area of electronic communications; protecting personal data and privacy; freely disseminating and gathering information; ensuring integrity and safety of public electronic telecommunication networks; ensuring the system for clear and reliable information and protection of users' interests. These are basic principles which are permeated over the electronic communication network.

300. A public electronic communications network is expected to enable: "free selection of carrier and terminal equipment, safe use, integrity of public electronic telecommunication network and interoperability of publicly available electronic communications services." As determined under the Decision on the identification of an operator with significant market power, use of the specific electronic communications network elements *inter alia* assumes the following activities: to negotiate in good faith with operators over the different issues in order to enable the access to network; to carry out the interconnection of electronic communications network; to grant free access to different protocols and other technologies; to provide adequate technical conditions for the electronic communication infrastructure; "to provide facilities necessary for interoperability of services for different types of services" (i.e., intelligent networks services) (Article 75).

Part IV. Cross Ownership Regulation

301. The issues on ownership in the Montenegrin national arena have been defined by several legal texts. The implementation of these acts is mainly monitored by two agencies: the Agency of Electronic Media, monitoring the transparency of ownerships and monopolies, and its potential misuses, and the Agency for protection of competition, established by the Government of Montenegro. The cross—ownership issues in media are regulated in the *legi generali* provisions of the Constitution of Montenegro and the Law on Prevention of Competition (LPC). Montenegro opts for market economy based on free entrepreneurship, competition, and free movement of goods, services, capital, labor, and employment. The Constitution of Montenegro, as stated in Article 93 paragraph 5, prohibits any kind of monopolistic behavior in the Montenegrin economic order. The article states that "any action or deed creating or encouraging monopolistic position on the market shall be contrary to the Constitution." Also, it states that freedom and pluralism of media shall be respected. The Law on Prevention of Competition similarly provides the basic rules on restrictive agreements, abuses of dominant positions and merger control, in accordance with the *acquis*. In the Screening report of Montenegro, Montenegro's anti-trust legislation is generally seen to be in line with the *acquis*.[138]

302. According to the LPC, competition in the Montenegrin market could be impaired by three instruments: agreements, abuse of a dominant position, and strengthening the concentration. Montenegrin law recognizes three models of its impairing effects: a model of preventing competition, a model of restricting competition, and a model on distorting competition. Thus, any preventing, restricting, or distorting competition via written, verbal, explicit, tacit agreement, or practice shall be prohibited and shall be null and void (Article 8). In other words, a dominant position in a market exists if it has no competitors or has significant market power enabling it to restrict or prevent development of effective competition in the market or a part of it. It also exists "if it has a significantly better position in relation to competitors enabling it to undertake business activities to a significant extent independently of its competitors, suppliers, buyers or end users" (Article 14). It is presumed that an undertaking has a dominant position in the market if its share exceeds 50% or if there is no significant competition between them and if their aggregate share in the relevant market exceeds 60%. Furthermore, the law stipulates three situations of undertakings: first, the merger of two or more independent undertakings or parts thereof in the relevant market; second, the acquisition, by one or more natural persons already controlling at least one undertaking, or by one or more undertakings, of indirect or direct control of the whole or a part of another undertaking; and third, "where two or more independent undertakings

138. Screening report Montenegro, Chapter 8 – Competition Policy, 2012, available at: http://ec.europa.eu/enlargement/pdf/montenegro/screening_reports/screening_report_montenegro_ch08.pdf.

establish a new undertaking or acquire joint control of the existing undertaking which operates independently on a lasting basis and performs all the functions of an autonomous undertaking" (Article 16).

303. Along with the general national laws, there are two specific legal acts defining the issue of cross-ownership in media: Media law (ML) and the Law of Electronic Media (LEM). Article 1 of the ML, Article 5 of Media law states that monopoly is not allowed in performing media activities. It further states that "the protection against monopolies in media activities shall be provided under separate law." Other than these general determinations, Media Law, as the main legislative piece, does not provide details regarding the print media ownership.[139] On the contrary, the Law on Electronic Media, since 2010, provides for the rules on ownership in electronic media.[140]

304. Regarding the question on broadcasting media ownership, the Law on Electronic Media (LEM) provides detailed regulations in part VIII, named "Protection of the electronic media pluralism and diversity," through three parts.

305. In the first place, LEM introduces obligations on ensuring transparency of ownership among the AVM service providers and related persons within AEM. Articles 129–130 define the obligations of the AVM service provider to inform AEM on a variety of data such as: name, head office/residence of natural and legal persons, the actual percentage of a share or stake of holders, the stake in other legal entities providing AVM services, and information on more than 10% share held by its owners in other legal entities providing AVM services in the given AVM service provider. The Law also defines the category of related persons, "which are mutually linked by management, capital or in some other way which enables them to jointly set business policy, operate in accord with the intention of attaining shared goals, or so that one person has the possibility of guiding another or to substantially affect their financial and business decisions, or decision on programme base of electronic media." These persons are: closer family members—parents, children, siblings, adoptive parents and children; persons related by marriage; close family members of the spouse; holders of a stake or share in business or other titles that give them right to participate in management of another entity with at least 20% of voting rights; the same person holds a stake or share in business or other titles that give them right to participate in management of another entity with at least 20% of voting rights in both legal entities; through a marketing or other agreement, when over three months or longer within one year they

139. Camovic, M., *Media Institute of Montenegro, Radno pravni status novinara u Crnoj Gori – NOVINARSTVO IZMEĐU STRAHA ZA EGZISTENCIJU*, Podgorica, 2015, available at: http://www.mminstitute.org/files/Izvjestaj%20radna%20prava%20MNE.pdf, p. 10 Media Institute report was based on research on the journalists' position in Montenegro, within the regional project on the Partnership for media Development in South East Europe. It has included the state institutions, such as Ministries and Agencies, as well as the media outlets working in Montenegro.

140. Brkic, D., *MEDIA Ownership and Financing in Montenegro: Weak Regulation Enforcement and Persistence of Media Control*, available at: http://www.mminstitute.org/files/Medijsko%20vlasnistvo%20i%20finansiranje%20medija%20u%20Crnoj%20Gori%20(1).pdf, pp. 10–12. Also *see* Agency of Electronic Media Decisions on cross-ownership in media, available at: http://www.ardcg.org/index.php?option=com_docman&task=cat_view&gid=29&dir=DESC&order=date&Itemid=26&limit=10&limitstart=200.

receive over 30% of advertising revenues; by being members of management bodies of a legal entity in which they perform this function and persons deemed as related persons with members of management bodies of that legal entity (Article 130).

306. Furthermore, LEM provides for the legal determination of the media concentration. It specifies that it exists when a broadcaster: "has a share in the founding capital of another broadcaster, a legal entity publishing a daily newspaper or a legal person performing the activity of an information agency or vice versa; concurrently holds several broadcasting licenses; concurrently broadcasts radio and television programme; concurrently broadcasts radio and/or television programme and publishes daily newspapers distributed within the area of the said radio and/or television programme coverage; concurrently broadcasts radio and/or television programme and pursues the activity of news agencies." It further specifies that media concentration also exists when "broadcaster's founders are natural or legal persons who are at the same time: founders of another broadcaster; founders of a legal person publishing a daily printed media within the area of radio or television programme coverage; founders of an information agency; spouses and common law spouses up to the second degree in the direct or side line of natural persons. If a broadcaster has a several licenses of AVM services it is obliged to keep separate accounts for them" (Article 131).

307. The Law is very specific regarding the determination of the unlawful media concentration. It provides that unlawful concentration exists when a broadcaster: "1) holding a licence for national coverage broadcasting: holds a stake in the founding capital of another broadcaster with such licence with more than 25% share of capital or voting rights, holds more than a 10% stake in the founding capital of a legal entity publishing daily print media with the circulation exceeding 3,000 copies, or vice versa, holds more than a 10% stake in the founding capital of a legal entity performing the activity of a news agency and vice versa, concurrently publishes the daily print media with the circulation exceeding 3,000 copies; 2) except the national public broadcaster, broadcasts over the same area more than one television and one radio programme with the same or similar programme base; 3) radio or television programme licensed for broadcasting with local or regional coverage: holds more than 30% stake in the founding capital of another broadcaster with regional or local coverage over the same area; concurrently, over the same or in neighbouring areas, publishes local daily print media" (Article 132 LEM).

308. This Law provides that unlawful media concentration also exists in the situation "where a natural person who is a founder of a broadcaster or a person who are his relatives in direct line up to the second degree or his spouse, holds a stake in the founding capital of another broadcaster, founder of a daily print media or news agency."

309. As a consequence of the unlawful media concentration, the granting of the license to operate can be rejected or revoked. AEM shall not grant a broadcasting license if its granting would lead to an unlawful media concentration. In fact, in the application procedure the applicant is obliged to submit a certified statement that no unlawful media concentration would occur with possible granting of the license. In case the AEM estimates that granting a license will trigger unlawful media concentration, it would order the broadcaster to rectify the irregularities within three months. If a broadcaster fails to act accordingly, AEM shall revoke their license (Article 134).

310. The Article 135 of LEM provides the obligation of notifying AEM of any changes in its ownership structure. In fact, any change in ownership structure exceeding a 10% share of the broadcaster requires previous prior written approval of Council.

311. The state's instrument in ensuring and fostering media pluralism and preservation of media diversity is the fund generated from a share of games of chance revenues. The procedure of the application process has been regulated by the Law on Games of Chance. LEM, in Article 136, specifies that this fund shall be used for: fostering production of commercial broadcaster programs of public interest — minorities' rights and persons with a hearing or visual disability and any other disabilities; prevention and combating all forms of discrimination; promotion of nature, environment and health; foster the culture of public dialogue and cultural creation; investment in science, art and education; preservation of Montenegrin national and cultural identity; fostering and promotion of human rights exercise and safeguarding; foster raising awareness of gender equality. The awarding funds procedure is strongly determined by the complexity, importance and the duration of the program production. On the other hand, these funds cannot be used for: retransmission of other stations' programs; purchased programs; reruns of own production; programs of own production for which broadcasters have provided coverage of costs from own revenues, donations, sponsorship, or grants by domestic and foreign institutions; programs already co-financed on any grounds from the Budget of Montenegro or budgets of local self — government units.

Part V. Supervision: Media Regulator

Chapter 1. Organization

312. In the Montenegrin national legal system, media regulators are present in the form of AEM and AECPS. Their functioning and organizations are mainly regulated by the two bylaws: Law on Electronic Media (LEM) and Law on Electronic Communications (LEC), Rulebook on the Programme Standards of the Electronic Media (RPSEM) and several decisions.

313. The AEM as an autonomous legal entity AVM service regulatory body with public authorities acting in the public interest. It shall be functionally independent from any state authority. Agency of the Electronic Media, as provided under the Articles 46–47 of the RPSEM, supervises the application of RPSEM under the principles specified in the document.

314. AEM has legislative power in producing AVM services and development program, developing plans for the use of the radio frequency band for designated for terrestrial broadcasting, developing radio frequency allocation plan for terrestrial broadcasting, and rendering opinions on the need to designate an operator with significant market power. The organization and tasks of the AEM are usually defined through the organization of its managing, organizational units. All Agency responsibilities and competencies are divided between the managing bodies: AEM Council and AEM Director (Article 13 of LEM).

315. The AEM Council, also has legislative competences for adopting some documents. The Council of Agency also gives opinions on plans for the use of the radio frequency band. It decides on granting the right to AVM service provision; approves temporary or permanent assignment, rental or otherwise transferal of AVM service provision license; adopts the rules on the amount, the method of calculation and payment of a registration fee and license fees for provision of AVM services; adopts rules on program standards for AVM service provision; adopts rules on requirements regarding minimum proportions reserved for European audiovisual works and independent productions, in line with European standards; adopts rules determining requirements and proportions reserved for ACC standards, defines the measures against AVM service providers and taking decisions as per complaints regarding their operation; decides as per appeals against AEM's first instance decisions; takes measures for temporary restrictions to the freedom of reception and retransmission of AVM services from other countries; reports to the European Commission in accordance with this Law and the ensuing implementing legislation; adopts Council's Rules of Procedure; elects the Chair from among the Council members; appoints and dismisses the AEM

Director; adopts the general legal act on internal organization and job systematization; adopts work plans, activity reports and periodic and annual accounts of AEM; adopts the financial plan for the coming year and the financial statements for the previous year; hires an independent certified auditor to audit final accounts of AEM; adopts other rules for implementing this Law; performs other tasks, as per the Law and the AEM Articles of Association. Also, Council is obliged, as specified under Article 15, to make publicly available within time limits the following documents: (1) AEM Activity Report for the previous year, focusing on the performance of responsibilities envisaged by law; (2) AEM Financial Report for the previous year, with the audit report from an authorized auditor (Article 14).

316. The AEM Director shall be appointed by the Council, following a public competition. Along with the general requirements stipulated by Labor law, the person eligible for the AEM director shall fulfill additional three conditions: (1) to be a Montenegrin national and reside in Montenegro; (2) hold a university degree; (3) have at least five years of work experience. The AEM Director shall: represent and act on behalf of the AEM; manage and guide the AEM work; be accountable to the Council; be responsible for the operation and regularity of AEM's work; propose a general act on AEM's internal organization and job systematization; propose AEM work plans; submit AEM activity reports and financial statements to the Council; propose a general act on minimum activity in case of staff being on strike; propose to the Council decisions on purchase, sale, and mortgaging of AEM's assets, as well as on taking bank loans and issuing financial guarantees; adopt the decision granting and revoking licenses for AVM services provision (Article 40).

317. In the same manner, the AECPS, is functioning as the independent authority in the area of electronic communications, since 2001.[141] The role of the AECPS is predominantly oriented on the fixed and mobile telephony market, internet and broadband access market, internet penetration market. The conditions for electronic communications are also in the focus of common work of these two agencies. Just as in the case of the Agency of Electronic Media, the Council and Director are the established bodies of the AECPS. The Agency is in charge of the Montenegrin electronic communication networks and its infrastructure, set up so that electronic communications services can be properly functioning.[142]

318. Although the Agency of Electronic Media is an independent regulatory body, some NGOs contest its role as an adequate monitoring capacity. For example, the Freedom House in its Report for 2015 states that media regulators "are not financially independent," though they are self-financed. Such observations have followed after the adoption of the amendments on LEM in 2013 which required the AEM to return budget surpluses to the state budget. That decision has affected the period of three years, from 2013 to 2016. Similar solutions have occurred in the functioning of the AECPS requiring Agency to return budget surpluses and thereby question its independent

141. Agency of Electronic Communications and Postal Services, Annual Report of 2014, available at: http://www.ekip2.me/download/izvjestaji/oradu/GI%202014%20-%2017%2009%20ENG%20VERZIJA%2022%2009.pdf.

142. For the analysis of the Serbian legal text *see* : Regulatorna Agencija Za Elektronske Komunikacije i Poštanske Usluge, Centar za primenjene evropske studije, 2014. *See* more on Country Report 2015, available at: https://freedomhouse.org/report/freedom-press/2015/montenegro.

status. The self-financing mechanism has been seen as the common solution in the regulatory agencies throughout the region.

319. In fact, licensing, registration and monitoring of the communication tools are predominantly handled by those two agencies. These agencies are also connected so that their main communications are aimed at: (1) expertly preparing and approving the plans of allocating radio-frequency bands; and (2) providing opinions to the regulatory authority for electronic communications on the need for operators with significant market power based on their analysis of the existence of non-competitive market of electronic communications services.

Chapter 2. Tasks

320. The main tasks of the media regulators on the Montenegrin media market process of supervision over the enforcement of obligations of AVM service providers is defined under the Chapter IX of the Law on Electronic Media. Supervision over the implementation of this Law shall be exercised by AEM which monitors whether AVM service providers adhere in all respects with the requirements from the license. With a view of implementing the competences envisaged by law, an AVM service provider is obliged, at AEM request, to make available all data, information, and documents needed for performing the regulatory function in this field, within the time set by AEM, which may not be shorter than seven days.

321. In exercising its monitoring and supervisory functions, AEM may order: (1) a broadcaster to: duly post a warning designating programs that may jeopardize the health, moral, intellectual, emotional, and social development of a child, show the name, symbol, or short identification sign of a radio or television program in compliance with the law, harmonize radio or television broadcasting with the license granted, enable the exercise of the right to short news, put a stop to prohibited political advertising, clearly indicate the ordering party in political advertising; (2) an on-demand AVM service provider to: "stop distributing programmes for which it does not hold an approval/contract, distribute radio and/or television programmes concurrently, wholly and unchanged, in compliance with the licence for on-demand AVM service provision and the approval of the programme right holder, adhere to the list of programmes included in the catalogue, stop distributing programmes violating programme standards set by Council, enable users access to network under equal terms."

322. As already stipulated AEM and AECPS are obliged to mutually cooperate and coordinate their work as regards radio frequencies allocated for AVM services. AEM shall cooperate with EKIP and all other administration bodies regulating the competition in electronic communications market analysis. Before deciding on granting a license for provision of AVM services, AEM may also exchange information with regulatory bodies of EU Member States on media service providers if radio or television broadcasting or provision of other AVM services concerns other EU Member States. AEM is expected to cooperate with counterpart regulatory bodies of other countries, with international experiences and standards. In coordination with competent state administration authorities, AEM shall cooperate with relevant international organizations. Before accepting international conventions and other instruments pertaining to provision of AVM services, responsible administration bodies are obliged to obtain the AEM's opinion.

323. The AECPS has a number of the competences regulated by Law on Electronic Communication. It's tasks are, *inter alia*, the following: adoption and implementation of the legislative pieces such Addressing Plan and Numbering Plan; Plan for allocation of radio-frequency spectrum and controls its implementation; Radio Frequency Assignment Plans, monitoring and coordinating of the radio-frequency spectrum; implementing the procedures for allocation of limited resources on non-discriminatory terms; maintaining the registers and databases; resolving users' complaints and disputes arising from the electronic communications market; determining the procedure for protection of interests and rights of users; monitoring the functioning of the Universal Service (administers the collection of fees paid for funding of the Universal Service and appoints its operator); monitoring of the work of operators and technical regulations and standards effective in Montenegro; professionally supervising the fulfillment of operators' obligation; cooperating with the other Montenegrin regulatory body such as Agency of Electronic Media and regulatory bodies of other countries; participating of the European and international organizations competent bodies and institutions; providing analyses of the relevant markets (operators with significant market power and preventing its negative effects), public opinion analysis and data on market development indicators (Article 11).

Chapter 3. Sanctioning Powers

324. As defined in the majority of the regional national legal systems, Montenegrin legal texts provide for two types of administrative supervision measures rendered by the Council. These are: warnings and temporary or permanent revocation of a license for an AVM service (Articles 140–143 of LEM).

325. As stated in the Article 140 "with a view of rectifying the irregularities noted, the AEM may issue a warning to the AVM service provider, and may also, temporarily or permanently, revoke broadcasting license or license for provision of on-demand AVM service." The decision on the measure shall be published in an adequate manner on the website. Also, a warning shall be issued to an AVM service provider for violation of an obligation stipulated by LEC, by AEM's legal act or in the license granted.

326. License for provision of an AVM service shall be temporarily revoked for thirty days, if the AVM service provider: "failed to start providing service in the time stipulated; failed to act in accordance with AEM's orders as regards compliance with the provisions of this Law governing unlawful media concentration; even after being issued a warning and pronounced a fine continues to violate provisions of this Law on program standards; even after being issued a warning fails to settle the annual license fee; as a non-for-profit broadcaster changes its status or if broadcasting ACC in contravention to the Legal solutions." The law also states that if an AVM service provider previously has issued the measure of temporary license revocation twice, the license shall be revoked permanently.

327. An AVM provider has the right to file an appeal against the administrative supervision measure with the Council that defers its execution, within fifteen days from being given the decision. A representative of the AVM service provider shall have the right to attend the Council session considering the appeal against the decision on temporary or permanent revocation of license. The provider is obliged to execute the final Council decision, and in case of failure to do so the involuntary enforcement procedure shall be conducted. An administrative dispute may be instigated against the Council decision upon appeal. Article 144 specifies that "a responsible official shall decide, within thirty days from complaint lodging, upon the complaint of a natural or a legal person regarding the operation of a provider." An appeal may be lodged with Council against the decision within fifteen days from the decision delivery. Council is obliged to pass the decision on appeal within fifteen days from it being lodged. LEM specifies that all issues, unless specified under this law, are defined under the Law on administrative procedure.

328. Similarly, the strongest power of the AECPS is its ability to revoke the approval for use of radio frequencies in the following situations: submission of the incorrect data during the application procedure; any non-compliance with the required conditions; non-removal of deficiencies within the time limit, not paying the fees for use of radio frequencies after Agency warning (Article 120 of the LEC).

329. In addition to it, Chapter X of LEM specifies the punitive provisions on misdemeanor offenses in seventy-three situations — grounds, which occur whenever legal person does not fulfill the legal obligations. Although AEM does not in fact,

Chapter X named Punitive provisions, names sanctioning power of the Agency of Electronic Media. There is the general prescribed provision providing that the legal person shall be punishable by a fine ranging from EUR 500 to EUR 6,000. The person held liable within a legal person shall be punishable by a fine ranging from EUR 100 to EUR 2,000.

330. Montenegrin law, according to the *numerus clausus* principle, strictly specifies the grounds for these offenses. We have grouped them into two categories: (1) substantial issues, and (2) technical issues.

331. Infringements of the technical aspect of the broadcasting are mainly, according to Article 146, related to the: (1) denial of a service user access to data on the name of AVM service provider, the registered office, or address, e-mail address, or web page of the AVM service provider; (2) failure to conduct fair prize competitions; (3) failure to legally transmit and organize cinematographic works and contracts; (4) failure to provide a due warning for programs which may impair physical, health, moral, mental, intellectual, emotional, and social development of minors; (5) transmission of the programs which: may impair physical, health, moral, mental, intellectual, emotional, and social development of minors, contain pornography, support violence, exploit credulity, failure to continuously display name, or identification sign of an electronic media throughout the television broadcasts; (6) failure to display name, symbol or short identification sign of an electronic media when retransmitting programs of other broadcasters; (7) failure to obtain AEM's approval before broadcasting significantly changed program structure; (8) advertising or teleshopping which are not readily recognizable; (9) uses data which may be misleading; (10) failure to clearly identify the ordering party in advertising. In this group of the reasons are also failures to: (a) set up and keep accounting for on-demand AVM services separate; (b) adequately obtain prior written approval of the rights holder; (c) distribute radio and/or television programs concurrently in compliance with the license granted; (d) adequately perform distribution of encoded satellite programs; (e) distribute, free of charge, programs of national public broadcasters; (f) notify on-demand AVM service providers in a timely fashion; (g) distribute programs for which the broadcaster does not hold a broadcasting right using a certain platform; (h) adhere to the list of radio or television programs included in the catalog; (j) notify AEM beforehand, in writing, of any change of radio or television programs; (k) distribute programs in compliance with set standards; (l) distribute programs via registered electronic communication network etc. (Article 146).

332. The breaches of substantial provisions are seen as a non-compliance with the defined program standards. This group of reasons are also listed as the "misdemeanour offences." Thus, the failure to broadcast at least twelve hours a day, to devote at least 10% of total weekly program to news and current affairs from the coverage zone, to broadcast news program lasting at least thirty minutes or within it at least one news not shorter than twenty minutes, to ensure European audiovisual works to make up at least 51% of its annual transmission time, to provide more than 10% share of audiovisual works of independent producers in annual transmission time or that at least half of such works are produced in the last five years, a failure to clearly mark radio or television program reruns, are seen as the legal grounds for the calling upon sanction powers. Additionally, use of exclusive rights purchased in such a way that a substantial proportion of the public in an EU Member State or a state party to the international treaty binding Montenegro is deprived of the possibility of following events of major importance for the society and which are in line with its domestic legislation designated for whole or partial live coverage, or where necessary or appropriate for objective reasons in the public interest, whole or partial deferred coverage on free television, in the capacity of a public broadcaster, the proportion of advertising spots exceeds 10% per clock hour, or if the proportion of advertising and teleshopping spots exceeds nine minutes within one clock hour during the day, in the capacity of a commercial broadcaster, the proportion of advertising spots exceeds 15% per clock hour, or if the proportion of advertising and teleshopping spots exceeds 20% within one clock hour during the day, shows advertising spots within religious contents, formal ceremonies, programs related to tragic events of wide scope or programs lasting thirty minutes or shorter, broadcasts sponsored AVM services or programs with their content or scheduling influenced by the sponsor or the sponsor affecting responsibility or editorial independence of the AVM service provider, broadcasts sponsored AVM services or programs directly encouraging the purchase or rental of goods or services, in particular by making special promotional references to those goods or services, fails to clearly identify sponsored AVM services and programs, broadcasts wholly or partially sponsored AVM services or programs not clearly identified by the name, logo, and/or other symbol of the sponsor such as a reference to its product(s) or service(s) or a distinctive sign thereof in an appropriate way for programs at the beginning, during and/or at the end of the programs, broadcasts AVM services or programs sponsored by legal and natural persons whose principal activity is the manufacture or sale of products or provision of services whose advertising is prohibited by law, broadcasts AVM services or programs sponsored by legal and natural persons whose activities include the manufacture or sale of medicinal products available only on prescription or medical procedures or treatments which are not compliant with a separate law governing health care, broadcasts sponsored news or current affairs programs, broadcasts programs sponsored by political parties, coalitions or other political organizations; shows a sponsorship logo during children's programs and religious programs; broadcasts audiovisual programs containing product placement without meeting the requirements, broadcasts programs with product placement with their content or scheduling influenced by the person placing the product or such a person affecting responsibility or editorial independence of the AVM service provider; broadcasts programs with product placement which directly encourage the purchase or rental of goods or services, in particular by making special promotional references to those goods or services or by giving prominence to the product; broadcasts programs with product placement without clearly informing viewers of product placement.

Selected Bibliography

Legal Texts (Decisions, National Laws, EU Laws)

Broadcasting Law (OG of MNE, Nos. 51/02, 62/02, 46/04, 56/04)
Constitution of Montenegro (OG of MNE, Nos. 01/07, 38/13)
Convention on Access to Official Documents
Council of Europe Strategy on the Rights of the Child 2012 – 2015, CM(2011)171 final, available at http://www.coe.int/t/DGHL/STANDARDSETTING/CDcj/StrategyCME.pdf
Council of Europe Convention on the Protection of Children against Sexual Exploitation and Sexual Abuse, July 12, 2007, CETS No.: 201, available at https://www.coe.int/en/web/conventions/full-list/-/conventions/treaty/201
Criminal Code (OG of MNE, No. 70/03, 13/04, 47/06, 40/08, 25/10, 32/11, 40/13, 56/13)
Criminal Code (OG of MNE, Nos. 70/03, 13/04, 47/06, 40/08, 25/10, 32/11, 64/11, 40/13, 56/13, 14/15)
Decision on the List of Events of Major Importance for the Public in Montenegro (OG of MNE, No. 11/12)
Decision on the List of Events of Major Importance for the Public in Montenegro (OG of MNE, No. 11/12)
Digital Broadcasting Law (OG of MNE, Nos. 34/11, 31/12)
Directive 2010/13/EU of the European Parliament and of the Council of March 10, 2010 on the coordination of certain provisions laid down by law, regulation or administrative action in Member States concerning the provision of audiovisual media services (Audiovisual Media Services Directive)
Electoral Law (OG of MNE, No. 4/98)
EUROPEAN Convention on Human Rights and Freedoms
European Convention on Human Rights and Fundamental Freedoms, available at http://www.echr.coe.int/Documents/Convention_ENG.pdf
Foreigners Law (OG of MNE, Nos. 82/2008 and 72/09)
Guidelines of the Committee of Ministers of the Council of Europe on child-friendly justice and their explanatory memorandum (Adopted by the Committee of Ministers on November 17, 2010 at the 1098th meeting of the Ministers' Deputies Guidelines and Explanatory memorandum - version edited May 31, 2011, available at: http://www.coe.int/t/dghl/standardsetting/childjustice/Guidelines%20on%20child-friendly%20justice%20and%20their%20explanatory%20memorandum%20_4_.pdf
International Covenant On Civil And Political Rights (ICCPR) *adopted by the United Nations General Assembly* on December 16, 1966, available at https://treaties.un.org/doc/publication/unts/volume%20999/volume-999-i-14668-english.pdf,

Journalists' Code of Ethics of 2016, available at http://www.osce.org/fom/255576?download=true
Labor Law (OG of MNE, Nos. 49/08, 26/09, 59/11 and 66/12)
Law on Accounting and Auditing (OG of MNE, Nos. 69/05, 80/08 and 32/11)
Law on Administrative Disputes (OG of MNE, No. 60/03)
Law on Amendments of Electoral Law (Law on Election of Councillors and Members) (OG of MNE, No. 04/98, 05/98, 17/98, 14/00, 18/00, 09/01, 41/02, 46/02, 45/04, 48/06, 56/06, 46/11, 14/14, 47/14).
Law on Bankruptcy and Liquidation of Insurance Companies (OG of MNE, No. 11/07)
Law on Bankruptcy Proceedings (OG of MNE, No. 11/0)
Law on Banks (OG of MNE, Nos. 17/08, 44/10, and 40/11)
Law on Business Organizations (OG of MNE, Nos. 06/02, 17/07, 80/08, 40/10, and 40/11)
Law on Central Bank (OG of MNE, Nos. 40/10, 46/10, and 6/13)
Law on Civil Procedure (OG of MNE, No. 22/04)
Law on Contract and Torts (OG of MNE, No. 47/08)
Law on Copyright and Related Rights (OG of MNE, No. 37/11)
Law on Courts (OG of MNE, No. 11/15)
Law on Criminal Procedure (OG of MNE, No. 79/09)
Law on Designations of Origin, Geographical Indications and Designations of Guaranteed Traditional Specialty Agricultural Products and Foodstuffs (OG of MNE, No. 18/11)
Law on Electronic Communications (OG of MNE, No. 40/13)
Law on Electronic Media (OG of MNE, Nos. 46/10, 40/11, 53/11, 055/16)
Law on Employment and Work of Foreigners (OG of MNE, Nos. 22/08 and 32/11)
Law on Enforcement and Guarantee (OG of MNE, No. 36/11)
Law on Financial Leasing (OG of MNE, No. 81/05)
Law on Financing of Political Parties (OF of MNE, Nos. 42/11, 60/11, 1/12)
Law on Financing Political Parties (OG of MNE, No. 49/08)
Law on Financing Political Subjects and Electoral Campaigning (OG of MNE, No. 52/14).
Law on Foreign Investment Law (OG of MNE, Nos. 82/08, 72/09, 32/11)
Law on Free Access to Information (OG of MNE, No. 44/12)
Law on Games of Chance (OG of MNE, Nos. 52/04, 13/07)
Law on General Administrative Procedure (OG of MNE, No. 60/03)
Law on Geographical Indications (OG of MNE, No. 48/08)
Law on Legal Protection of Industrial Designs (OG of MNE, No. 27/13)
Law On Liability Of Legal Entities For Criminal Offenses (OG of MNE, No. 70/03, 13/04)
Law on media (OG of RS, Nos. 83/*2014*, 58/2015 i 12/2016), available at http://www.parlament.gov.rs/upload/archive/files/cir/pdf/zakoni/2014/2511-14.pdf
Law on Ownership Rights (OG of MNE, No. 19/09)
Law on Patents (OG of MNE, Nos. 66/08 and 49/11)
Law on Political Parties (OG of MNE, Nos. 21/04, 73/10, 40/11, 59/11)
Law on Prevention of Illegal Businesses (OG of MNE, No. 29/13)
Law on Prohibition of Discrimination (OG of MNE, No. 18/2014)
Law on Protection of Competition (OG of MNE, No. 44/12)

Selected Bibliography

Law on Protection of Topographies of Integrated Circuits (OG of MNE, No. 75/10)
Law on Public Procurement (OG of MNE, No. 42/11)
Law on Public Service Broadcasting of Montenegro
Law on Public Services Broadcasting of Montenegro (OG of MNE, Nos. 79/08, 45/12, 054/16)
Law on Ratification of the European Convention on Transfrontier Television (OG of MNE, No. 01/08)
Law on Takeover of Joint Stock Companies (OG of MNE, No. 18/11)
Law on the Election of the President of Montenegro (OG of MNE, Nos. 17/07, 08/09)
Law on the Prevention of Conflict of Interests (OG of MNE, No. 01/09)
Law on the Protection of Personal Data (OG of MNE, Nos. 79/08 and 70/09)
Law on Torts and Obligations (OG of MNE, No. 47/07)
Law on Trademarks (OG of MNE, No. 72/10)
Media Law (OG of MNE, Nos. 82/08, 51/02, 362/02)
Resolution on Rules for Political Parties' Representation in Public Media Founded by State During the Election Campaign (OF of MNE, No. 4/98)
Rulebooks on Audiovisual Commercial Communications (OG of MNE, No. 36/11)
Rulebooks on Conditions on Determining Programme Standards in Its Own Production (OG of MNE, No. 46/12...)
Rulebooks on Programme Standards in Electronic Media (OG of MNE, Nos. 46/10, 007/16)
Statute of the Agency for Electronic Media (OG of MNE, No. 46/10)
The Beijing Rules — the United Nations Standard Minimum Rules for the Administration of Juvenile Justice, adopted by General Assembly resolution 40/33 of November 29, 1985, available at http://www.ohchr.org/Documents/ProfessionalInterest/beijingrules.pdf.
Vilnius Recommendations on Safety of Journalists, CIO.GAL/111/11 June 8, 2011, available at http://www.osce.org/cio/78522?download=true

Case Law

Barfod v. Denmark, ECtHR Judgement (February 22, 1989) Application No. 11508/85
Bladet Tromso and Stensaas v. Norway ECtHR Judgement (May 22, 1999) Application No. 21980/93
Castells v. Spain, ECtHR Judgement (April 13, 1992), Application No. 11798/85
Delfi AS v. Estonia, ECtHR Judgement (June 16, 2015) Application No. 64569/09
Filipovic v. Serbia, ECtHR Judgement (November 20, 2007) Application No. 27935/05
Gulati & Ors v. MGN Limited, ECtHR Judgement (May 21, 2015) Application No. EWHC 1482 (Ch)
Independent News and Media and Independent Newspapers v. Ireland, ECtHR Judgement (June 16, 2005) Application No. 55120/00
Koprivica v. Montenegro, ECtHR Judgement (November 22, 2011) Application No. 41158/09
Krone Verlag GmbH v. Austria, ECtHR Judgement (June 19, 2012) Application No. 27306/07
Lingens v. Austria, ECtHR Judgement (July 8, 1986) Application No. 9815/82

Lopes Gomes da Silva v. Portugal, ECtHR Judgement (September 28, 2000) Application No. 37698/97
Magyar Tartalomszolgáltatók Egyesülete and Index.hu Zrt v. Hungary (February 2, 2016) Application No. 22947/13
Maronek v. Slovakia, ECtHR Judgement (April 19, 2001), Application No. 32686/96
MGN Limited v. the United Kingdom, ECtHR Judgement (June 12, 2012) Application No. 39401/04
Mladina v. Slovenia, ECtHR Judgement (April 17, 2014) Application No. 20981/10
Morar v. Romania, ECtHR Judgement (July 7, 2015) Application No. 25217/06
Oberschlick v. Austria (No. 2), ECtHR Judgement (July 1, 1997) Application No. 20834/92
Oberschlick v. Austria, ECtHR Judgement (May 23, 1985) Application No. 11662/85
Pakdemirli v. Turkey, ECtHR Judgement (February 22, 2005), Application No. 35839/97
Pavel Karpov v. Bill Browder, High Court of Justice Judgement (October 14, 2013) Application Nos. HQ12DO3133 and HQ12DO1742
Sabanovic v. Montenegro and Serbia, ECtHR Judgement (May 13, 2011) Application No. 5995/06
Şener v. Turkey, ECtHR Judgement, (July 18, 2000), Application No. 26680/95
Steel and Morris v. the United Kingdom, ECtHR Judgement (May 15, 2005) Application No. 68416/01
Subotic v. Knezevic, High Court of Justice Judgement (October 14, 2013) Application No. HQ11DO3680
Sunday Times v. The United Kingdom ECtHR Judgement (April 26, 1979) Application No. 6538/74
Supreme Court Opinion on the meaning and the scope of the free access to the court decisions, Bulletin 2011, The Supreme Court of Montenegro, ISNN 1800-5810
Tolstoy Miloslavsky v. United Kingdom, ECtHR Judgement (July 13, 1995), Application No. 18139/91

Legal Doctrine

Allan, S., News Culture, Open University Press, London, 2004.
Amponsah, P., Libel Law, Polical Criticism, and Defamation of Public Figures, LFB Scholarly Publishing LLC, New York, 2004.
Assange, J., The Banality of Don't Be Evil, New York Times, 2013, available at: http://www.nytimes.com/2013/06/02/opinion/sunday/the-banality-of-googles-dont-be-evil.html?pagewanted=all&_r=0.
Azar, D., "On Selecting Jurisdiction in Internet Defamation Cases", *Common Law Review* (2013): 7. http://www.commonlawreview.cz/on-selecting-jurisdiction-in-internet-defamation-cases.
Baird, J., Assange as Tyrant, New York Times, 14 September, 2013, available at: http://www.nytimes.com/2013/09/15/opinion/sunday/assange-as-tyrant.html.
Bal, F., Moć medija, Clio, Beograd, 1997.
Barendt, E. et al., Media Law: Text, Cases and Materials, Pearson Education Limited, Harlow, England, 2014.

Selected Bibliography

Barendt, E. et al., Libel and the Media: The Chilling Effect, Clarendon Press, Oxford, 1997.

Barendt, E., Freedom of Speech. Second ed. Oxford University Press, New York, 2005.

Barnett, S., "Public Interest - Public Decide", *British Journalism Review* 23, No. 2 (2012), available at: http://www.bjr.org.uk/data/2012/no2_barnett.

Bell, A., Libel Tourism- International Forum Shopping for Defamation Claims. Center for Public Affairs, Jerusalem, 3–9, 2008, available at: http://jcpa.org/wp-content/uploads/2011/09/libeltourism.pdf.

Belmas G., Overbeck, W., Major Principles of Media Law, California State University, Fullerton, 2014.

Bennett, L.W., News: The Politics of Illusions, University of Washington, 2012.

Berg, H., Istraživačko novinarstvo, Clio, Beograd, 2007.

Bernett, S., Journalism, Democracy and Public Interest: Rethinking Media for the Digital Age, University of Oxford, Reuters Institute, September, 2009.

Blumler J.G., Gurevitch, M., The Crisis of Public Communication, Routledgde, London and New York, 1995.

Bona, M., Towards The "Europeanisation" Of Personal Injury Compensation: Contexts, Tools, Projects, Materials And Cases On Personal Injury Approximation in Europe, published in Personal Injury Compensation in Europe, Bona M., Mead, P., Kluwer, Deventer, 2003.

Brigs, A., Berg, P., Društvena istorija medija, Clio, Beograd, 2006.

Brigs, A., Koblli, P., Uvod u studije medija, Clio, Beograd, 2005.

Brkic, D., Media Ownership and Financing in Montenegro: Weak Regulation Enforcement and Persistence of Media Control, available at: http://www.mminstitute.org/files/Medijsko%20vlasnistvo%20i%20finansiranje%20medija%20u%20Crnoj%20Gori%20(1).pdf.

Camovic, M., Media Institut of Montenegro, Radno pravni status novinara u Crnoj Gori – NOVINARSTVO IZMEĐU STRAHA ZA EGZISTENCIJU, Podgorica, 2015, available at: http://www.mminstitute.org/files/Izvjestaj%20radna%20prava%20MNE.pdf).

Cassidy, J., Why Edward Snowden Is a hero, New Yorker, 2013, available at: http://www.newyorker.com/online/blogs/johncassidy/2013/06/why-edward-snowden-is-a-hero.html.

Chaiken, M., Poll: Americans Say WikiLeaks Harmed Public Interest; Most Want Assange Arrested, Washington Post, 14th of December, 2010, available at: http://www.washingtonpost.com/wp-dyn/content/article/2010/12/14/AR2010121401650.html.

Chihaia, G.N., Short Essay on Presumption of Innocence. ECHR Precedent, available at:http://www.wseas.us/e-library/conferences/2011/Brasov1/LAW/LAW-29.pdf.

Članak: Finansirati javni interes, a ne medija, Medijski centar Srbije, available at: http://www.mc.rs/finansirati-javni-interes-a-ne-medije.50.html?eventId=58197.

Collins, M., 2005. The Law of Defamation and the Internet. (Second edn). Oxford University Press, Canada.

Collins, M., 2014. After the Defamation Act, London May No Longer Be the Libel Capital of the World. http://www.democraticaudit.com/?p=2150.

Čomski, N, Kontrola medija, Rubikon, Beograd, 2011.

Cooper G., Whittle, S., Privacy, Probity and Public Interest, Reuters Institute for the Study of Journalism, 2008.
David, E., Svennevig, M.M., The Public Interest, the Media and Privacy, BBC, March 2002.
Davies, N., Perspective: Libel Law: Repressing Journalists in Uk and Phl, 2014, available at: https://julienealega.wordpress.com/tag/journalists/.
De Berg, H., Istraživačko novinarstvo, Clio, Beograd, 2007.
De Hert, P. Gutwirth, S., Privacy, Data Protection and Law Enforcement: Opacity of the Individual and Transparency of Power, available at: http://works.bepress.com/cgi/viewcontent.cgi?article=1004&context=serge_gutwirth, 2006.
Dej, L.A., Etika u medijima, Primeri i kontroverze, Medija centar, Beograd Plus, Beograd 2004.
Dutertre, G., Izvodi iz sudske prakse - Evropski sud za ljudska prava, Bemust, Sarajevo, 2002.
Edvard S. H. i Mekčesni, R.V., Globalni mediji, Clio, Beograd, 2004.
Entman, R.M., Democracy Without Citizens: Media and the Decay of American Politics, Oxford University Press, Oxford, 1989.
FitzGibbon, D., Stumping for the Rule of Law in the Footsteps of the Commissars. Res Gestae, 55, 2011.
Forest, H., 1996, Wisdom Tales from Around the World. Little Rock. August House Publishers, Arkansas.
Forest, H., Wisdom Tales from Around the World, Little Rock. August House Publishers, Arkansas, 1996.
Freedom of expression in Europe, Case-law concerning Article 10 of the European Convention on Human Rights Council of Europe, Strasbourg Cedex, Updated edition, March, 2007.
Gelatt, T. A., "The People's Republic of China and the Presumption of Innocence", *Journal of Criminal Law and Criminology* 73 (Spring 1982).
Glasser, C., International Libel and Privacy Handbook, Bloomberg Press, New York, 2006.
Gocini, Dj., Istorija novinarstva, Clio, Beograd, 2001.
Guardian, http://www.theguardian.com/media/2013/oct/15/libel-tourism-high-court-karpov-subotic-foreign-sue, 2015.
Halliday, J., O'Carroll, L., "Libel Tourism at an End, Say Lawyers Following the High Court Decisions." The Harding, L., Dosije Snouden, Evro Giunti Beograd, Beograd, 2014.
Holmes, D., Communication Theory: Media, Technology and Society, Sage Publications, London, 2005.
Hopsers, J., Libertaniasm: A Political Philosophy for Tomorrow, Nash Publishing, Los Angeles, CA, 1971.
http://www.academia.edu/3632045/Journalism_Ethics_Publics_Right_to_Know_versus_Infringement_of_Privacy.
http://www.theguardian.com/books/2014/mar/06/julian-assange-publisher-defence-wikileaks.

Selected Bibliography

Hulin, A., "Joint Declarations of the Representatives of Intergovernmental Bodies to Protect Free Media and Expression." OSCE The Representative on Freedom of the Media. Vienna, 29 (2013) http://www.osce.org/fom/99558?download=true.

Hulnick, G., Media Ethics: Defining the Line of a Privacy, Sheldon Chumir Foundation for Ethics in Leadership, available at: http://www.gailhulnick.com/published_articles.html, 2001.

Human rights files, Case law concerning Article 10 of the European Convention of Human rights, Council of Europe, 2001.

Jantol, T., Politička javnost, Birotisak, Zagreb, 2004.

Johnston, D., The General Influence of Roman Institutions of State and Public Law. http://iuscivile.com/legacy/reprints/j-1.pdf, 1997.

Kendrick, L., "Speech, Intent and the Chilling Effect", *William & Mary Law Review* 54 (2013): 1633. http://scholarship.law.wm.edu/wmlr/vol54/iss5/4.

Kent, M. R., William, L.E., The Law of Public Communication (Eighth edition), Pearson Education, 2010.

Kenyon, A., Defamation - Comparative Law and Practice, Faculty of Law University of Melbourne, Australia, 2006.

Kenyon, A., Richardson, M., New Dimension in Privacy Law, Cambridge University Press, New York, 2006.

Kenyon, A., TV Futures - Digital Television Policy in Australia, Melbourne University Press, Victoria, 2007.

Kider, R., Etičke dileme, CID, Podgorica, 2006.

Kin, Dz., Mediji i demokratija, Filip Višnjić, Beograd, 1995.

Kovač, B., Rozenstil, T., Elementi novinarstva, Institut za medije Crne Gore, CID, Podgorica, 2006.

Kovačič, M.P., Što je novinarska etika? // Medijska istraživanja: znanstveno-stručni časopis za novinarstvo i medije, 1998.

Krejg, R., Onlajn novinarstvo, Clio, Beograd, 2010.

Lakočević, B., Pažin, Z., Bulatović, R., Mićunović, V., Vuković, D., Ivanović, A., Vodič za novinare kroz krivični postupak, Podgorica: CEDEM, OSCE, 2010.

Laksmiwardan, A., Journalism Ethics Public's Right to Know versus Infringement of Privacy, available at:Andy Coulson jailed for 18 months over phone hacking, BBC, available at: http://www.bbc.com/news/uk-28160626

Leach, P., Taking a Case to the European Court of Human Rights, Oxford University Press, London, 2005.

Lej, L.A., Etika i mediji, Medija centar, Beograd, 2004.

Levmore, S., Nussbaum, M., The Offensive Internet: Speech, Privacy, and Reputation, Harvard University Press, Cambridge, MA, 2011.

Linden, C.G., "Focusing on Growth: Innovation, the Media and Public Interest", University of Helsinki, Innovation of Journalism, 2009.

Lorimer, R., Masovne komunikacije, Clio, Beograd, 1998.

Macovei, M., Freedom of expression, Council of Europe, 2001.

Malović, S., Mediji i društvo, ICEJ, Zagreb, 2007.

Malović, S., Osnove novinarstva, Golden marketing – Tehnička knjiga, Zagreb, 2005.

Malović, S., Ricchiardi, S., Vilović, G., *Etika novinarstva*, Izvori, Zagreb, 1998.

Marija Vidić, Guru hakerskih svetih ratnika, Vreme, 2010, available at:*http://www.vreme.com/cms/view.php?id=965994.*
McPhail, T., Global Communication: Theories, Stakeholders and Trends, Blackwell Publishing, Malden & Oxford, 2006.
Melkonian, H., Defamation, Libel Tourism and Speech Act of 2010, Cambria press, Amherst, 2011.
Mendel, T., Sloboda izražavanja: Vodič za tumačenje člana 10 Evropske konvencije.
Mening, B., Heroj ili izdajnik, Politika, mart 2013, available at: http://www.politika.rs/rubrike/Svet/Bredli-Mening--heroj-ili-ili-izdajnik.lt.html.
Middleton, R.K., Lee, E.W., The Law of Public Communication (Eight edition), Pearson Education, 2010.
Mirosavljević, M., Vilović, G., Kunczik, M., Istraživačko novinarstvo, Amosgraf, Sarajevo, 2009.
Murdok, Dz., Sloboda misli savesti i veroispovesti, Vodič za primjenu člana 9 Evropske konvencije o ljudskim pravima, Savet Evrope, Beograd, 2008.
Murray, C., Edward Snowden, The European Convention on Human Rights and State Surveillance, Human Rights Is Ireland, 17 July, 2013, available at: http://humanrights.ie/civil-liberties/edward-snowden-the-european-convention-on-human-rights-and-state-surveillance/.
Nikic, S., Mediji i ljudska prava, Sloboda izražavanja, Presude Evropskog suda za ljudska prava, Beograd, 2006.
Nikolić, D., Medijsko pravo, Službeni glasnik, Beograd, 2010.
Nikšić, S. (Ed.), Sloboda izražavanja, Centar za profesionalizaciju medija, 2006.
Nolasco, C., Spaic A., Cenzura kao odgovor na (ne) etičko izvještavanje medija, ZBORNIK – Vjerodostojnost medija – nedostižan san, Montenegrin Academy of Science and Art, ISBN 978-86-7215-389-7, p. 39- 51, January, 2017.
Nolasco, C., Spaić, A., Novović, M., Mugosa, N., Libel Tourism in the Light of the Most Recent UK cases, available at https://medijskidijalozi.files.wordpress.com/2014/12/medijski-dijlozi-br-20.pdf.
Nolasco, C., Spaic, A., Vaughn MS, "Media Access to Juvenile Proceedings: Balancing the Tightrope Between Privacy Rights and Freedom of the Press", *International Journal of Law, Crime and Justice* 43, no. 4, 643–675.
Nolasco, C., Spaic, A., Vaughn, M., "Legal Standards Governing Media Access to Delinquency Proceedings: Balancing the Tightrope Between Privacy Rights and Freedom of the Press", *International Journal of Law, Crime and Justice* (March 2015), available at: http://www.sciencedirect.com/science/article/pii/S1756061615000373.
O'Carroll, L., Coulson A., "Turned News of the World into a Criminal Enterprise", The Guardian, available at:http://www.theguardian.com/uk-news/2014/jun/30/andy-coulson-news-world-phone-hacking-trial.
Ossowska, M., "Moral and Legal Norms", *The Journal of Philosophy*, 57 (1960).
Pažin, Z., Građansko-pravni aspekt zaštite prava ličnosti i slobode medija, OEBS, Podgorica, 2014. Vacić, Z. Etika javne riječi u medijima i politici, Centar za liberalno – demokratske studije, Beograd, 2004.
Phillip, A., Should President Obama Pardon Edward Snowden, ABC News, 20th of December, 2013, available at: http://abcnews.go.com/blogs/politics/2013/12/should-president-obama-pardon-edward-snowden/.

Selected Bibliography

Rawls, J., Justice and Fairness: A Restatement, Harvard University Press, London, 2001

Renucci, J., Introduction to the European Convention on Human Rights Council of Europe, June 2005.

Ribičić C., Ljudska prava i ustavna demokratija. Ustavni sud Srbija i Službeni glasnik Srbije, Beograd, 2012.

Ribičić, C., & Kaučić, I., Constitutional Limits of Legislative Referendum: The case of Slovenia. http://www.jus.uio.no/english/research/news-and-events/events/conferences/2014/wccl-cmdc/wccl/papers/ws16/w16-ribicic-kaucic.pdf, 2014.

Richardson, J., Bellanger, F., Legal Cases, New Religious Movements and Minority Faiths. Ashgate Publishing Limited, England, 2014.

"Right to know", Article 19, available at: http://www.article19.org/data/files/pdfs/standards/righttoknow.pdf.

Robinson, C., In Defence of Julian Assange, The Guardian, 6th of March 2014, available at: https://www.theguardian.com/books/2014/mar/06/julian-assange-publisher-defence-wikileaks

Rolf, D., Defamation Law, Thomson Reuters, Australia, 2015.

Rolf, D., et al., Media Law: Cases, Materials and Commentary, Oxford University Press, Australia and New Zealand, 2015.

Rolph, D., Reputation, Celebrity and Defamation Law, Ashgate, Aldershot, UK, 2008.

Rols, Dz., Prava naroda, Narodna knjiga ALFA, 2001

Rosen, J., "The Right to Be Forgotten", *Stanford Law Review*, 64 (2012) http://www.stanfordlawreview.org/sites/default/files/online/topics/64-SLRO-88.pdf.

S. Smet, "Freedom of Expression and the Right to Reputation: Human Rights in Conflict", *American University International Law Review* 26, no. 1 (2010).

Scheer, R., Obama Should Thank and Pardon Edward Snowden, The National, 29 October, 2013, available at: http://www.thenation.com/article/176873/obama-should-thank-and-pardon-edward-snowden.

Shankland, S., 2010. Execs Convicted in Google Video Case in Italy, http://www.cnet.com/news/execs-convicted-in-google-video-case-in-italy-20000092/ (accessed 3 March 2016).

Shankland, S., 2010. Execs Convicted in Google Video Case in Italy, http://www.cnet.com/news/execs-convicted-in-google-video-case-in-italy-20000092/ (accessed 3 March 2016).

Šil, Dz., Afera prisluškivanja telefona u Velikoj Britaniji, Akademija za diplomatiju i bezbjednost, 2014, arhiva, available at:http://www.diplomatija.com/sr/1597/news/afera-prislu%C5%A1kivanja-telefona-u-velikoj-britaniji-jonathan-schell-%C4%8Dak-ni-staljin-nije-prislu%C5%A1kivao-mrtve-naredna-faza-bila-je-zata%C5%A1kavanje/.

Sinanović, A., Društvena odgovornost medija, Udruženje Vesta, 2007, available at: http://www.vesta.ba/images/publikacije/Drustvenaodgovornostmedija.pdf.

Skoko, B., Bajs, D., Objavljivanje nesitina i manipuliranje činjenicama u hrvatskim medijima i mogućnosti zaštite privatnosti, časti i ugleda, Politička misao (2007).

Smet, S., "Freedom of Expression and the Right to Reputation: Human Rights in Conflict", *American University International Law, Review* 26, no. 1 (2010).

Snowden, E., If I Could Go Anywhere That Place Would Be Home, The Guardian, 29th of May, 2014, available at: http://www.theguardian.com/world/2014/may/29/edward-snowden-interview-breaking-law-was-only-option-says-whistleblower.

Spaić, A., Mediji zbog senzacionalizma, profita i politike ili zbog nas?, Media Dialogues, Godina VII Broj 20, Podgorica, Novembar 2014, ISSN 1800-7074 COBISS.CG - ID 12734480, available at https://medijskidijalozi.files.wordpress.com/2014/12/medijski-dijlozi-br-20.pdf.

Spaic, A., "Autonomy and Antidiscrimination in Private Law." In *Civil Law Forum for South East Europe, Collection of Sudies and Analyses,* Edited by N. Reich, C. Jessel-Holst, & T. Josipovic. Skopje: Deutsche Gesellschaft fur Technische Zusammenarbeit, 2014.

Spaic, A., et al., "Decriminalization of Defamation - The Balkans Case a Temporary Remedy or a Long Term Solution?", *International Journal of Law, Crime and Justice* (2016), http://dx.doi.org/10.1016/j.ijlcj.2016.05.002.

Spaić, A., Media Coverage in Minor Proceeding: In the Light of Krone Case of ECHR, Godina VII Broj 13-14, Podgorica Novembar 2012, ISSN 1800-7074 COBISS.CG - ID 12734480, available at: https://medijskidijalozi.files.wordpress.com/2013/02/md-broj-13-14.pdf.

Spaic, A., Novovic, M., "Commercial and Economic Law in Montenegro (National Monograph)", ISBN 9789065449429, Kluwer Law International, Alphen aan den Rijn, The Netherlands, 2014.

Sullivan, D., Libel Tourism, Silencing the Press Through Transnational Legal Treats, Center for International Media Assistance, Washington D.C, 2010.

Sykes, G., Courting the Media. Contemporary Perspectives on Media & Law, 2011.

Taylor, P.M., Global Communications, International Affairs and the Media Since 1945, Routledge, London and New York, 1997

Vilović, G., Etički prijepori u Globusu i Nacionalu 1999–2000., Zagreb 2004.

Vodinelic, V., Pravo masmedija, Beograd 2003.

Vučinić, N., Osnovi ljudskih prava i sloboda, CID, Podgorica, 2001

Vuković, S., "Udar na privatnost može izazvati jaču kontrolu medija", NUNS, Dosije o medijima 34 "News of the world", available at:http://dosije.nuns.rs/dosije-34/News-of-the-World.

White, P.A., "The Justification of Education", In *The Philosophy of Education.* Edited by R.S. Peters. Oxford: Oxford University Press, 1987, Peščanik.net, available at: http://pescanik.net/2012/02/obrazovanje-demokratija-i-javni-interes/.

Žižek, S., How Wikileaks Opened Our Eyes to the Illusion of Freedom, The Guardian, 19.jun 2014, available at: http://www.theguardian.com/commentisfree/2014/jun/19/hypocrisy-freedom-julian-assange-wikileaks.

Other

Agency of Electronic Media, Annual Report of 2015, available at: http://www.ardcg.org/index.php?option=com_docman&task=cat_view&gid=43&Itemid=26.

Article 19, Defending the freedom of expression and information. https://www.article19.org/.

Selected Bibliography

Bilteni NVO Akcije za ljudska prava: Sloboda izražavanja, available at: http://www.hraction.org/?page_id=459#bilteni_si.

CCE, Equal chances with all media outlets in Montenegro, CGO, 2015, available at: phttp://media.cgo-cce.org/2014/12/cgo-cce-jednake-sanse-za-sve-medije-u-CG-2014.pdf, CCE, How much and to whom do the citizens of Montenegro pay for advertising?, 2012 available at: http://media.cgo-cce.org/2015/12/cgo-cce-how-much-and-to-whom-do-the-citizens-in-mne-pay-for-adv.pdf.

CCE, How much, to which media and related agencies did municipalities in Montenegro pay for their services, 2012, available at: http://media.cgo-cce.org/2015/12/cgo-cce-how-much-to-which-media-and-related-agencies-did-municipalities-in-mne-pay-for-their-services.pdf.

CCE, How much, to which media and related agencies did municipalities in Montenegro pay for their services, 2013, available at: http://media.cgo-cce.org/2015/12/cgo-cce-how-much-and-to-whom-do-the-citizens-in-mne-pay-for-adv-2012.pdf.

CEDEM and OSCE, Socijalni položaj novinarske profesije u Crnoj Gori, November 2014, available at: http://sindikatmedija.me/images/pdf/osceizvjestaj.pdf.

CEDEM, Mapping of the Anti-discrimination Legal, Institutional and Policy Framework in Turkey and the Western Balkans. Country Report: Montenegro.

Clemency for Edward Snowden? The public is sceptical, Washington Post, 2 January, 2014, available at: http://www.washingtonpost.com/blogs/the-fix/wp/2014/01/02/clemency-for-edward-snowden-the-public-is-skeptical/.

Civil Registration and the Prevention of Statelessness: a Survey of Roma, Ashkaelia and Egyptians in Montenegro, United Nations High Commissioner Refugees – UNHCR and United Nations Children's Fund – UNICEF, May 2009.

CODE OF GOOD PRACTICE Guidelines and Explanatory Report adopted by the Venice Commission, at its 52nd Session, Opinion No. 190/2002, CDL-AD (2002) 23 rev Or. Fr.,available at whttp://www.venice.coe.int/webforms/documents/default.aspx?pdffile=CDL-AD(2002)023rev-e.

European parliament kills call to protect Edward Snowden, World Socialist Web Site, 13. February, 2014, available at: http://www.wsws.org/en/articles/2014/02/13/snow-f13.html.

Evropski sud za ljudska prava, Godišnji izvještaj, 2005.

Journalism - Democracy - Public interest, Reuters, 2008, available at: https://reutersinstitute.politics.ox.ac.uk/fileadmin/documents/Publications/Journalism_Democracy___Public_Interest_for_website.pdf.

MIPA, Montenegro Country Report 2011, available at:http://www.mipa.co.me/userfiles/file/MIPA%20Country%20report%202011%20web.pdf, February 15, 2014.

MIPA, Montenegro Country Report Edition 2015 available at: http://www.mipa.co.me/dcs/MIPA-Country-Report-2015-web.pdf.

Montenegro 2013 International Religious Freedom Report, available at: www.state.gov/documents/orhanization/222461.pdf.

Montenegro 2013 International Religious Freedom Report, available at: www.state.gov/documents/orhanization/222461.pdf.

Montenegro Progress Report, Enlargement Strategy and Main Challenges 2014-2015, COM(2014) 700 final.

National Human Development Report 2009 Montenegro: Society for All (NHDR), United Nations Development Programme (UNDP) in Montenegro, 2009, available at *http://www.undp.org.me/home/actualities/NHDR.pdf.*
OSCE. OSCE welcomes Montenegro's decriminalization of speech offences, 2011. http://www.osce.org/montenegro/80808.
Pravo na zaborav moći će da koriste moćnici da prepravljaju istoriju, Politika, maj 2014, available at: http://www.politika.rs/rubrike/spektar/Digitalni-svet/Pravo-na-zaborav-koristice-mocnici-da-prepravljaju-istoriju.lt.html.
Rasna netrpeljivost i "govor mržnje": međunarodni i hrvatski standardi i praksa, Centar za ljudska prava, Zagreb, 2004.
Razumevanje ljudskih prava, Priručnik o obrazovanju za ljudska prava, Ministarstvo za ljudska i manjinska prava Srbije i Crne Gore, Beograd, 2005.
Report of the Special Rapporteur on the promotion and protection of the right to freedom of opinion and expression, Frank La Rue, United Nations General Assembly, A/HRC/26/30/Add.1, Distr.: General 29 April 2014, available at https://www.crin.org/sites/default/files/freedomofexpression_2.pdf.
Results of the 2011 census are available at: http://www.monstat.org/ (website of the National Bureau of Statistics or Monstat).
Screening report Montenegro Chapter 10Information society and media, available at http://ec.europa.eu/enlargement/pdf/montenegro/screening_reports/screening_report_montenegro_ch10.pdf.
Snowden Revelations, Al Jazeera, 2012, available at:http://america.aljazeera.com/articles/multimedia/timeline-edward-snowden-revelations.html.
The Swedish Bar Association and the New York City Bar Association, Independent Legal Mission to Study Press Freedom in Montenegro, May 2013, available at: http://www2.nycbar.org/pdf/report/uploads/Montenegro.pdf.
UNESCO: International Bureau of Education, Emile Durkheim, vol. 23, no. 1/2, 1993, International Bureau of Education, 2001, available at: http://www.ibe.unesco.org/fileadmin/user_upload/archive/publications/ThinkersPdf/durkheie.pdf.
Vlada Crne Gore, Kancelarija zastupnika Crne Gore pred Evropskim sudom za ljudska prava, Odbrane presude Evropskog suda za ljudska prava 2, Podgorica, 2011.
Vodič za tumačenje člana 10 Evropske konvencije o ljudskim pravima i njegovog konteksta, Savet Evrope, Kancelarija u Beogradu, 2014, available at: http://www.coe.org.rs/def/.

Index

The numbers here refer to paragraph numbers.

Index

Index